isaiah

the book of

isaiah

authorised king james version

printed by authority

published by canongate

with an introduction by | peter ackroyd

First published in Great Britain in 1999
by Canongate Books Ltd
14 High Street, Edinburgh EH1 1TE

10 9 8 7 6 5 4 3 2 1

British Library Cataloguing-in-Publication Data
A catalogue record is available on request from
the British Library

ISBN 0 86241 970 0

Typeset by Palimpsest Book Production
Book design by Paddy Cramsie at et al
Printed and bound in Great Britain
by Caledonian International, Bishopbriggs

a note about pocket canons

The Authorised King James Version of the Bible, translated between 1603–11, coincided with an extraordinary flowering of English literature. This version, more than any other, and possibly more than any other work in history, has had an influence in shaping the language we speak and write today.

Twenty-four of the eighty original books of the King James Bible are brought to you in this series. They encompass categories as diverse as history, philosophy, law, poetry and fiction. Each Pocket Canon also has its own introduction, specially commissioned from an impressive range of writers, to provide a personal interpretation of the text and explore its contemporary relevance.

introduction by peter ackroyd

Peter Ackroyd's most recent books include bestselling biographies of Dickens *(1990),* Blake *(1995) and* Thomas More *(1998), and the novels* Dan Leno and the Limehouse Golem *(1994) and* Milton in America *(1996). He is the winner of a Somerset Maugham Award, the Guardian Fiction Prize, the Whitbread Prize for Biography and the prestigious James Tait Black Memorial Prize. He lives in London.*

We must approach this sacred text with great respect, doubting the ability of our mind to comprehend it and of our tongue to describe it. The book of *Isaiah* is not the work of one writer or one prophet but, like the Homeric epics, incorporates the voices of many authors in a tradition of oral poetry. Yet even though it comprises various sources its shape, like a river made out of many streams, is fluent and harmonious. Within its 66 chapters passages of lyrical melody are pressed up against words of prophetic force, moments of vision vouchsafed beside occasions for denunciation; the narrative combines stories, poems, descriptions, revelations and lamentations. It is, in little, representative of the Bible itself.

The origins of the various texts, original or interpolated, date variously from the eighth to the sixth century BCE. Yet in a book where history and poetry mingle, for devotional or ritual purposes, there is no need to attempt to locate a substratum of real or observable fact; just as the original documents have long since crumbled to dust, so we cannot sift the episodes concerning forgotten battles and distant kings.

The composition of the book itself is more certain – chapters 1 to 39 are the work of several authors, but all moving within a realm concerning prophecies of redemption as well as fierce polemic against pagan idolaters and the profligate among the Lord's own people. The 40th chapter marks the beginning of the work of the 'Deutero-Isaiah', perhaps the single most eloquent and inspiring of all the biblical writers who within 15 verses offers a vision of hope and of redemption for the people of Israel at the same time as, in a magnificent panegyric, he launches an attack upon Babylon and all the powers of this world. The third part, verses 55 to 66, acts as a coda to the first two sections, where interpolated hands have provided passages of prophecy and eschatology.

Harmony itself is achieved through the introduction of very clear formal preoccupations, together with an abiding and overriding concern for rhetorical elaboration and amplitude. Scholars of the Hebrew text, for example, have enumerated instances of alliteration and onomatopoeia designed expressly to lift a cadence or emphasise a phrase. The construction of the phrase itself is of the utmost significance, where simplicity and force work together in unison. That is why some of the lines from *Isaiah* have entered folk memory beyond the tribes of Israel – 'and they shall beat their swords into plowshares (2:4) … For unto us a child is born, unto us a son is given (9:6) ... The wolf also shall dwell with the lamb, and the leopard shall lie down with the kid (11:6) ... How art thou fallen from heaven, O Lucifer, son of the morning! (14:12) ... Let us eat and drink; for tomorrow we shall die (22:13) ... All flesh is grass (40:6) ... There is no peace, saith my God, to the wicked' (57:21) ... No rest for the wicked. The provenance of some of these phrases is disputed as not springing from the lips of the 'historical' Isaiah, but their relevance and influence are not in dispute. These are words which have literally changed the consciousness of the world.

Yet they are important, too, in maintaining the urgency and relevance of a narrative which speaks to many nations concerning the central aspirations of humankind. That is also why the economy and brevity of *Isaiah* allow a single phrase to denote the passage of many years or the history of one city. The utter simplicity of the author's voice emerges in passages of perfect pitch and power – 'Then shalt thou call [upon the Lord] ..., and he shall say, "Here I am." (58:9). Here I am. It is as if the whole world resounded with God's voice, and we may recall here William Blake's visionary conversation with Isaiah – 'I saw no God nor heard any,' the prophet informed the poet, 'in a finite organical perception; but my senses discover'd the infinite in everything.'

This in fact is one of the glories of *Isaiah*, where the grandeur or ineffability of the 'infinite' is expressed in terms of a local landscape or a specific activity, so that 'the burden of the valley of vision' (22:1) can be carried by details of weaving or of threshing. Here the aspiration towards the infinite and the illimitable is combined with a very clear and articulate presentation of contemporary realities. Israel is 'a lodge in a garden of cucumbers' (1:8), and the Lord tells Isaiah to walk towards 'the end of the conduit of the upper pool in the highway of the fuller's field' (7:3). The Lord shall tread down Moab 'even as straw is trodden down for the dunghill' (25:10) and will put forth his hands 'as he that swimmeth spreadeth forth his hands to swim' (25:11). *Isaiah* celebrates a universe in which the particulars of the social and natural world are revealed as tokens of spiritual activity, where world and spirit do indeed become one, like the swimmer, in a living pulse of energy – 'for the earth shall be full of the knowledge of the Lord, as the waters cover the sea' (11:9).

The economy of effect, together with the use of repetition, renders these sacred verses not unlike the texts of Anglo-Saxon poetry – or, indeed, the expression of any bardic people. The recitation may even have been accompanied by music, so that the whole narrative becomes a kind of performance in which the aspirations of both orator and audience alike are embodied. No one can ignore, either, the dramatic aspects of Isaiah where, for example, the anonymous author proclaims the fate of one unhappy man – 'He is despised and rejected of men; a man of sorrows, and acquainted with grief' (53:3). This has often been characterised as a prophecy of Christ's passion, yet it is more appropriately and less anachronistically seen as a most dramatic and human revelation of the outcast. In that sense, like the rest of *Isaiah*, it becomes a story of universal significance rather than a sample of pre-Christian revelation.

There has been much discussion, in recent years, of the

Bible as a literary rather than a sacred or historical text. Certainly the narrative devices are clear, with affiliations to western poetry and fiction. There is, for example, satire approaching an almost Swiftian vision of disgust at the flesh, in the description of the women of Zion 'with stretched forth necks and wanton eyes, walking and mincing as they go, and making a tinkling with their feet' (3:16), or in the depiction of the priests of Ephraim so drunk that 'all tables are full of vomit and filthiness' (28:8). But there are other forms of narrative in place here, as mysterious and as melodious as anything in epic poetry – 'And the posts of the door moved at the voice of him that cried, and the house was filled with smoke' (6:4). 'And his heart was moved, and the heart of his people, as the trees of the wood are moved with the wind' (7:2). 'For the heavens shall vanish away like smoke, and the earth shall wax old like a garment' (51:6).

Coleridge once remarked, of cadences like this, that the first chapter of *Isaiah* might be 'reduced to complete hexameters ... so true is it that wherever passion was, the language became a sort of metre'. In truth the words of *Isaiah* are neither prose nor poetry but, rather, a series of incandescent utterances which effortlessly find their true form. That is why the question of whether this is a poetic rather than a sacred text is redundant – there is no necessary distinction between the two since the highest poetry is always a manifestation of the sacred, while the most sacred insights will necessarily take on the vesture of poetry.

As such the effect of *Isaiah* upon European literature has been extensive and profound; its plangent combination of prophetic passages, with visionary epiphanies and lyrical enchantments, have affected the understanding of epic and pastoral as well as the nature of poetry itself. It stands out like a great melody, informing the future and irradiating the past.

the book of the prophet isaiah

The vision of Isaiah the son of Amoz,
    which he saw concerning Judah and Jerusalem
        in the days of Uzziah, Jotham, Ahaz,
    and Hezekiah, kings of Judah.
² Hear, O heavens, and give ear, O earth;
    for the Lord hath spoken,
        I have nourished and brought up children,
    and they have rebelled against me.
³ The ox knoweth his owner,
    and the ass his master's crib,
        but Israel doth not know,
    my people doth not consider.
⁴ Ah sinful nation, a people laden with iniquity,
    a seed of evildoers,
        children that are corrupters:
    they have forsaken the Lord,
        they have provoked
    the Holy One of Israel unto anger,
        they are gone away backward.
⁵ Why should ye be stricken any more?
    Ye will revolt more and more:
        the whole head is sick,
    and the whole heart faint.

⁶ From the sole of the foot even unto the head
   there is no soundness in it;
      but wounds, and bruises,
   and putrifying sores:
      they have not been closed, neither bound up,
   neither mollified with ointment.
⁷ Your country is desolate,
   your cities are burned with fire;
      your land, strangers devour it
   in your presence,
      and it is desolate, as overthrown by strangers.
⁸ And the daughter of Zion is left
   as a cottage in a vineyard,
      as a lodge in a garden of cucumbers,
   as a besieged city.
⁹ Except the Lord of hosts had left unto us
   a very small remnant,
      we should have been as Sodom,
   and we should have been like unto Gomorrah.
¹⁰ Hear the word of the Lord, ye rulers of Sodom;
   give ear unto the law of our God,
      ye people of Gomorrah.
¹¹ To what purpose is the multitude of
   your sacrifices unto me? saith the Lord:
      I am full of the burnt offerings of rams,
   and the fat of fed beasts;
      and I delight not in the blood of bullocks,
   or of lambs, or of he goats.

¹² When ye come to appear before me,
    who hath required this at your hand,
        to tread my courts?
¹³ Bring no more vain oblations;
    incense is an abomination unto me;
        the new moons and sabbaths,
    the calling of assemblies, I cannot away with:
        it is iniquity, even the solemn meeting.
¹⁴ Your new moons and your appointed feasts
    my soul hateth;
        they are a trouble unto me;
    I am weary to bear them.
¹⁵ And when ye spread forth your hands,
    I will hide mine eyes from you;
        yea, when ye make many prayers,
    I will not hear;
        your hands are full of blood.
¹⁶ Wash you, make you clean;
    put away the evil of your doings
        from before mine eyes; cease to do evil;
¹⁷ learn to do well; seek judgment,
    relieve the oppressed, judge the fatherless,
        plead for the widow.
¹⁸ Come now, and let us reason together, saith the Lord:
    though your sins be as scarlet,
        they shall be as white as snow;
    though they be red like crimson,
        they shall be as wool.

¹⁹ If ye be willing and obedient,
　　ye shall eat the good of the land;
²⁰ but if ye refuse and rebel,
　　ye shall be devoured with the sword,
　　　　for the mouth of the Lord
　　hath spoken it.
²¹ How is the faithful city become an harlot!
　　It was full of judgment;
　　　　righteousness lodged in it;
　　but now murderers.
²² Thy silver is become dross,
　　thy wine mixed with water.
²³ Thy princes are rebellious,
　　and companions of thieves:
　　　　every one loveth gifts,
　　and followeth after rewards:
　　　　they judge not the fatherless,
　　neither doth the cause of the widow
　　　　come unto them.
²⁴ Therefore saith the Lord, the Lord of hosts,
　　the mighty One of Israel,
　　　　Ah, I will ease me of mine adversaries,
　　and avenge me of mine enemies.
²⁵ And I will turn my hand upon thee,
　　and purely purge away thy dross,
　　　　and take away all thy tin.
²⁶ And I will restore thy judges as at the first,
　　and thy counsellors as at the beginning:

afterward thou shalt be called,
'The city of righteousness, the faithful city.'
²⁷ Zion shall be redeemed with judgment,
and her converts with righteousness.
²⁸And the destruction of the transgressors
and of the sinners shall be together,
and they that forsake the Lord
shall be consumed.
²⁹ For they shall be ashamed of the oaks
which ye have desired,
and ye shall be confounded for the gardens
that ye have chosen.
³⁰ For ye shall be as an oak whose leaf fadeth,
and as a garden that hath no water.
³¹And the strong shall be as tow,
and the maker of it as a spark,
and they shall both burn together,
and none shall quench them.

2   The word that Isaiah the son of Amoz saw
concerning Judah and Jerusalem.
²And it shall come to pass in the last days,
that the mountain of the Lord's house shall be
established in the top of the mountains,
and shall be exalted above the hills;
and all nations shall flow unto it.

³And many people shall go and say,
Come ye, and let us go up
to the mountain of the Lord,
to the house of the God of Jacob;
and he will teach us of his ways,
and we will walk in his paths:
for out of Zion shall go forth the law,
and the word of the Lord from Jerusalem.
⁴And he shall judge among the nations,
and shall rebuke many people,
and they shall beat their swords
into plowshares,
and their spears into pruninghooks:
nation shall not lift up sword against nation,
neither shall they learn war any more.
⁵O house of Jacob,
come ye,
and let us walk in the light of the Lord.
⁶Therefore thou hast forsaken thy people
the house of Jacob,
because they be replenished from the east,
and are soothsayers like the Philistines,
and they please themselves
in the children of strangers.
⁷Their land also is full of silver and gold,
neither is there any end of their treasures;
their land is also full of horses,
neither is there any end of their chariots.

⁸ Their land also is full of idols;
   they worship the work of their own hands,
      that which their own fingers have made.
⁹ And the mean man boweth down,
   and the great man humbleth himself:
      therefore forgive them not.
¹⁰ Enter into the rock,
   and hide thee in the dust,
      for fear of the Lord
   and for the glory of his majesty.
¹¹ The lofty looks of man shall be humbled,
   and the haughtiness of men
      shall be bowed down,
   and the Lord alone shall be exalted
      in that day.
¹² For the day of the Lord of hosts shall be upon
   every one that is proud and lofty,
      and upon every one that is lifted up;
   and he shall be brought low:
¹³ and upon all the cedars of Lebanon,
   that are high and lifted up,
      and upon all the oaks of Bashan,
¹⁴ and upon all the high mountains,
   and upon all the hills that are lifted up,
¹⁵ and upon every high tower,
   and upon every fenced wall,
¹⁶ and upon all the ships of Tarshish,
   and upon all pleasant pictures.

¹⁷And the loftiness of man shall be bowed down,
 and the haughtiness of men shall be made low:
  and the Lord alone shall be exalted
 in that day.
¹⁸And the idols he shall utterly abolish.
¹⁹And they shall go into the holes of the rocks,
 and into the caves of the earth,
  for fear of the Lord,
 and for the glory of his majesty,
  when he ariseth to shake terribly the earth.
²⁰In that day a man shall cast his idols of silver,
 and his idols of gold,
  which they made each one for himself
 to worship,
  to the moles and to the bats;
²¹to go into the clefts of the rocks,
 and into the tops of the ragged rocks,
  for fear of the Lord,
 and for the glory of his majesty,
  when he ariseth to shake terribly the earth.
²²Cease ye from man, whose breath is in his nostrils,
 for wherein is he to be accounted of?

3 For, behold, the Lord, the Lord of hosts,
 doth take away from Jerusalem and from Judah
  the stay and the staff,

the whole stay of bread,
and the whole stay of water,
² the mighty man, and the man of war,
the judge, and the prophet,
and the prudent, and the ancient,
³ the captain of fifty, and the honourable man,
and the counsellor, and the cunning artificer,
and the eloquent orator.
⁴And I will give children to be their princes,
and babes shall rule over them.
⁵And the people shall be oppressed,
every one by another,
and every one by his neighbour:
the child shall behave himself
proudly against the ancient,
and the base against the honourable.
⁶ When a man shall take hold of his brother
of the house of his father, saying,
'Thou hast clothing, be thou our ruler,
and let this ruin be under thy hand.'
⁷ In that day shall he swear, saying,
'I will not be an healer;
for in my house is neither bread nor clothing:
make me not a ruler of the people.'
⁸ For Jerusalem is ruined, and Judah is fallen,
because their tongue and their doings
are against the Lord,
to provoke the eyes of his glory.

⁹ The shew of their countenance
     doth witness against them;
          and they declare their sin as Sodom,
     they hide it not. Woe unto their soul!
          For they have rewarded evil unto themselves.
¹⁰ Say ye to the righteous,
     that it shall be well with him,
          for they shall eat the fruit of their doings.
¹¹ Woe unto the wicked! It shall be ill with him,
     for the reward of his hands shall be given him.
¹² As for my people,
     children are their oppressors,
          and women rule over them. O my people,
     they which lead thee cause thee to err,
          and destroy the way of thy paths.
¹³ The Lord standeth up to plead,
     and standeth to judge the people.
¹⁴ The Lord will enter into judgment
     with the ancients of his people,
          and the princes thereof:
     for ye have eaten up the vineyard;
          the spoil of the poor is in your houses.
¹⁵ 'What mean ye that ye beat my people to pieces,
     and grind the faces of the poor?'
          saith the Lord God of hosts.
¹⁶ Moreover the Lord saith,
     Because the daughters of Zion are haughty,
          and walk with stretched forth necks

and wanton eyes,
   walking and mincing as they go,
   and making a tinkling with their feet,
¹⁷ therefore the Lord will smite with a scab the crown
   of the head of the daughters of Zion,
      and the Lord will discover their secret parts.
¹⁸ In that day the Lord will take away the bravery
   of their tinkling ornaments about their feet,
      and their cauls,
   and their round tires like the moon,
¹⁹ the chains, and the bracelets,
   and the mufflers,
²⁰ the bonnets, and the ornaments of the legs,
   and the headbands, and the tablets,
      and the earrings,
²¹ the rings, and nose jewels,
²² the changeable suits of apparel,
   and the mantles, and the wimples,
      and the crisping pins,
²³ the glasses, and the fine linen,
   and the hoods, and the vails.
²⁴ And it shall come to pass,
   that instead of sweet smell there shall be stink;
      and instead of a girdle a rent;
   and instead of well set hair baldness;
      and instead of a stomacher
   a girding of sackcloth;
      and burning instead of beauty.

²⁵ Thy men shall fall by the sword,
    and thy mighty in the war.
²⁶ And her gates shall lament and mourn;
    and she being desolate
        shall sit upon the ground.

4   And in that day seven women
        shall take hold of one man, saying,
            We will eat our own bread,
        and wear our own apparel:
            only let us be called by thy name,
        to take away our reproach?
² In that day shall the branch of the Lord
    be beautiful and glorious,
        and the fruit of the earth shall be excellent
        and comely for them that are escaped of Israel.
³ And it shall come to pass,
    that he that is left in Zion,
        and he that remaineth in Jerusalem,
    shall be called holy,
        even every one that is written
    among the living in Jerusalem,
⁴ when the Lord shall have washed away
    the filth of the daughters of Zion,
        and shall have purged the blood of Jerusalem

from the midst thereof by the spirit of judgment,
    and by the spirit of burning.
⁵And the Lord will create upon every dwelling place
    of mount Zion,
        and upon her assemblies,
    a cloud and smoke by day,
        and the shining of a flaming fire by night:
    for upon all the glory
        shall be a defence.
⁶And there shall be a tabernacle for a shadow
    in the daytime from the heat,
        and for a place of refuge,
    and for a covert from storm
        and from rain.

5   Now will I sing to my wellbeloved
        a song of my beloved touching his vineyard.
            My wellbeloved hath a vineyard
        in a very fruitful hill.
    ²And he fenced it, and gathered out the stones thereof,
        and planted it with the choicest vine,
            and built a tower in the midst of it,
        and also made a winepress therein:
            and he looked that it should bring forth grapes,
        and it brought forth wild grapes.

³And now, O inhabitants of Jerusalem,
   and men of Judah,
      judge, I pray you, betwixt me and my vineyard.
⁴What could have been done more to my vineyard,
   that I have not done in it?
      Wherefore, when I looked
      that it should bring forth grapes,
         brought it forth wild grapes?
⁵And now go to;
   I will tell you what I will do to my vineyard:
      I will take away the hedge thereof,
   and it shall be eaten up;
      and break down the wall thereof,
   and it shall be trodden down.
⁶And I will lay it waste:
   it shall not be pruned, nor digged;
      but there shall come up briers and thorns:
   I will also command the clouds
      that they rain no rain upon it.
⁷For the vineyard of the Lord of hosts
   is the house of Israel,
      and the men of Judah his pleasant plant:
   and he looked for judgment,
      but behold oppression;
   for righteousness, but behold a cry.
⁸Woe unto them that join house to house,
   that lay field to field, till there be no place,
      that they may be placed alone

in the midst of the earth!

⁹ In mine ears said the Lord of hosts,
Of a truth many houses shall be desolate,
even great and fair, without inhabitant.

¹⁰ Yea, ten acres of vineyard shall yield one bath,
and the seed of an homer shall yield an ephah.

¹¹ Woe unto them that rise up early in the morning,
that they may follow strong drink;
that continue until night,
till wine inflame them!

¹² And the harp, and the viol, the tabret,
and pipe, and wine, are in their feasts but they
regard not the work of the Lord,
neither consider the operation of his hands.

¹³ Therefore my people are gone into captivity,
because they have no knowledge:
and their honourable men are famished,
and their multitude dried up with thirst.

¹⁴ Therefore hell hath enlarged herself,
and opened her mouth without measure:
and their glory, and their multitude,
and their pomp,
and he that rejoiceth, shall descend into it.

¹⁵ And the mean man shall be brought down,
and the mighty man shall be humbled,
and the eyes of the lofty shall be humbled.

¹⁶ But the Lord of hosts shall be exalted in judgment,
and God that is holy

shall be sanctified in righteousness.
¹⁷ Then shall the lambs feed after their manner,
and the waste places of the fat ones
shall strangers eat.
¹⁸ Woe unto them that draw iniquity with cords of vanity,
and sin as it were with a cart rope,
¹⁹ that say, 'Let him make speed, and hasten his work,
that we may see it,
and let the counsel of the Holy One of Israel
draw nigh and come,
that we may know it!'
²⁰ Woe unto them that call evil good, and good evil;
that put darkness for light,
and light for darkness;
that put bitter for sweet,
and sweet for bitter!
²¹ Woe unto them that are wise in their own eyes,
and prudent in their own sight!
²² Woe unto them that are mighty to drink wine,
and men of strength to mingle strong drink,
²³ which justify the wicked for reward,
and take away the righteousness
of the righteous from him!
²⁴ Therefore as the fire devoureth the stubble,
and the flame consumeth the chaff,
so their root shall be as rottenness,
and their blossom shall go up as dust,
because they have cast away

the law of the Lord of hosts,
   and despised the word of the Holy One of Israel.
²⁵ Therefore is the anger of the Lord
   kindled against his people,
      and he hath stretched forth his hand
   against them,
      and hath smitten them;
   and the hills did tremble, and their carcases
      were torn in the midst of the streets.
   For all this his anger is not turned away,
      but his hand is stretched out still.
²⁶ And he will lift up an ensign to the nations from far
   and will hiss unto them
      from the end of the earth:
   and, behold, they shall come with speed swiftly.
²⁷ None shall be weary nor stumble among them;
   none shall slumber nor sleep;
      neither shall the girdle of their loins
   be loosed,
      nor the latchet of their shoes be broken:
²⁸ whose arrows are sharp, and all their bows bent,
   their horses' hoofs shall be counted like flint,
      and their wheels like a whirlwind.
²⁹ Their roaring shall be like a lion,
   they shall roar like young lions: yea,
      they shall roar, and lay hold of the prey,
   and shall carry it away safe,
      and none shall deliver it.

³⁰And in that day they shall roar against them
    like the roaring of the sea:
        and if one look unto the land,
    behold darkness and sorrow,
        and the light is darkened
    in the heavens thereof.

6 In the year that king Uzziah died I saw also
    the Lord sitting upon a throne, high and lifted up,
        and his train filled the temple.
²Above it stood the seraphims:
    each one had six wings;
        with twain he covered his face,
    and with twain he covered his feet,
        and with twain he did fly.
³And one cried unto another, and said,
    'Holy, holy, holy, is the Lord of hosts:
        the whole earth is full of his glory.'
⁴And the posts of the door moved
    at the voice of him that cried,
        and the house was filled with smoke.
⁵Then said I, 'Woe is me! for I am undone;
    because I am a man of unclean lips,
        and I dwell in the midst of a people
    of unclean lips,
        for mine eyes have seen the King,
    the Lord of hosts.'

⁶ Then flew one of the seraphims unto me,
　　having a live coal in his hand,
　　　　which he had taken with the tongs
　　from off the altar.
⁷ And he laid it upon my mouth, and said,
　　'Lo, this hath touched thy lips;
　　　　and thine iniquity is taken away,
　　and thy sin purged.'
⁸ Also I heard the voice of the Lord, saying,
　　'Whom shall I send, and who will go for us?'
　　　　Then said I, 'Here am I; send me.'
⁹ And he said, 'Go, and tell this people;
　　"Hear ye indeed, but understand not;
　　　　and see ye indeed, but perceive not."
¹⁰ Make the heart of this people fat,
　　and make their ears heavy, and shut their eyes;
　　　　lest they see with their eyes,
　　and hear with their ears,
　　　　and understand with their heart,
　　and convert, and be healed.'
¹¹ Then said I, 'Lord, how long?'
　　And he answered, 'Until the cities be wasted
　　　　without inhabitant,
　　and the houses without man,
　　　　and the land be utterly desolate,
¹² and the Lord have removed men far away,
　　and there be a great forsaking
　　　　in the midst of the land.

¹³ But yet in it shall be a tenth, and it shall return,
and shall be eaten, as a teil tree, and as an oak,
whose substance is in them,
when they cast their leaves.'
So the holy seed shall be
the substance thereof.

7 And it came to pass in the days of Ahaz the son
of Jotham, the son of Uzziah, king of Judah,
that Rezin the king of Syria,
and Pekah the son of Remaliah, king of Israel,
went up toward Jerusalem to war against it,
but could not prevail against it.
² And it was told the house of David, saying,
'Syria is confederate with Ephraim.'
And his heart was moved,
and the heart of his people,
as the trees of the wood are moved
with the wind.
³ Then said the Lord unto Isaiah,
'Go forth now to meet Ahaz, thou,
and Shear-jashub thy son,
at the end of the conduit of the upper pool
in the highway of the fuller's field;
⁴ and say unto him, "Take heed, and be quiet;
fear not, neither be fainthearted
for the two tails of these smoking firebrands,

for the fierce anger of Rezin with Syria,
and of the son of Remaliah."
⁵ Because Syria, Ephraim, and the son of Remaliah,
have taken evil counsel against thee, saying,
⁶ "Let us go up against Judah, and vex it,
and let us make a breach therein for us,
and set a king in the midst of it,
even the son of Tabeal"'.'
⁷ Thus saith the Lord God,
'It shall not stand, neither shall it come to pass.
⁸ For the head of Syria is Damascus,
and the head of Damascus is Rezin;
and within threescore and five years
shall Ephraim be broken,
that it be not a people.
⁹ And the head of Ephraim is Samaria,
and the head of Samaria is Remaliah's son.
If ye will not believe,
surely ye shall not be established.'
¹⁰ Moreover the Lord spake again unto Ahaz, saying,
¹¹ 'Ask thee a sign of the Lord thy God;
ask it either in the depth,
or in the height above.'
¹² But Ahaz said,
'I will not ask, neither will I tempt the Lord.'
¹³ And he said, Hear ye now, O house of David;
is it a small thing for you to weary men,
but will ye weary my God also?

¹⁴ Therefore the Lord himself shall give you a sign.
Behold, a virgin* shall conceive, and bear a son,
and shall call his name Immanuel.
¹⁵ Butter and honey shall he eat,
that he may know to refuse the evil,
and choose the good.
¹⁶ For before the child shall know to refuse the evil,
and choose the good,
the land that thou abhorrest shall be forsaken
of both her kings.
¹⁷ The Lord shall bring upon thee,
and upon thy people,
and upon thy father's house,
days that have not come,
from the day that Ephraim
departed from Judah;
even the king of Assyria.'
¹⁸ And it shall come to pass in that day,
that the Lord shall hiss for the fly that is in
the uttermost part of the rivers of Egypt,
and for the bee that is in the land
of Assyria.
¹⁹ And they shall come, and shall rest all of them
in the desolate valleys,
and in the holes of the rocks,
and upon all thorns,
and upon all bushes.
²⁰ In the same day shall the Lord shave

* A young women

with a razor that is hired, namely,
    by them beyond the river,
by the king of Assyria,
    the head, and the hair of the feet;
and it shall also consume the beard.
[21] And it shall come to pass in that day,
    that a man shall nourish a young cow,
        and two sheep;
[22] And it shall come to pass,
    for the abundance of milk
        that they shall give he shall eat butter,
    for butter and honey shall every one eat
        that is left in the land.
[23] And it shall come to pass in that day,
    that every place shall be,
        where there were a thousand vines
    at a thousand silverlings,
        it shall even be for briers and thorns.
[24] With arrows and with bows
    shall men come thither;
        because all the land shall become briers
    and thorns.
[25] And on all hills that shall be digged
    with the mattock,
        there shall not come thither the fear of briers
    and thorns:
        but it shall be for the sending forth of oxen,
    and for the treading of lesser cattle.

8

Moreover the Lord said unto me,
'Take thee a great roll, and write in it
with a man's pen concerning
Maher-shalal-hash-baz.'
[2] And I took unto me faithful witnesses to record,
Uriah the priest, and Zechariah
the son of Jeberechiah.
[3] And I went unto the prophetess;
and she conceived, and bare a son.
Then said the Lord to me,
Call his name Maher-shalal-hash-baz.
[4] For before the child shall have knowledge to cry,
'My father', and 'My mother',
the riches of Damascus
and the spoil of Samaria
shall be taken away
before the king of Assyria.
[5] The Lord spake also unto me again, saying,
[6] Forasmuch as this people refuseth the waters
of Shiloah that go softly,
and rejoice in Rezin and Remaliah's son,
[7] now therefore, behold, the Lord bringeth up upon
them the waters of the river,
strong and many, even the king of Assyria,
and all his glory:
and he shall come up over all his channels,
and go over all his banks:
[8] and he shall pass through Judah;

he shall overflow and go over,
    he shall reach even to the neck;
and the stretching out of his wings
    shall fill the breadth of thy land,
O Immanuel.
⁹Associate yourselves, O ye people,
    and ye shall be broken in pieces;
        and give ear, all ye of far countries:
    gird yourselves, and ye shall be broken in pieces;
        gird yourselves,
    and ye shall be broken in pieces.
¹⁰Take counsel together, and it shall come to nought;
    speak the word, and it shall not stand,
        for God is with us.
¹¹For the Lord spake thus to me with a strong hand,
    and instructed me that I should not walk
        in the way of this people, saying,
¹²Say ye not, 'A confederacy',
    to all them to whom this people shall say
        'A confederacy';
    neither fear ye their fear, nor be afraid.
¹³Sanctify the Lord of hosts himself;
    and let him be your fear,
        and let him be your dread.
¹⁴And he shall be for a sanctuary;
    but for a stone of stumbling and for a rock
        of offence to both the houses of Israel,
    for a gin and for a snare
        to the inhabitants of Jerusalem.

¹⁵And many among them shall stumble, and fall,
and be broken, and be snared,
and be taken.
¹⁶Bind up the testimony,
seal the law among my disciples.
¹⁷And I will wait upon the Lord,
that hideth his face from the house of Jacob,
and I will look for him.
¹⁸Behold, I and the children
whom the Lord hath given me
are for signs and for wonders in Israel
from the Lord of hosts,
which dwelleth in mount Zion.
¹⁹And when they shall say unto you,
'Seek unto them that have familiar spirits,
and unto wizards that peep, and that mutter:
should not a people seek unto their God?
For the living to the dead?
²⁰to the law and to the testimony':
if they speak not according to this word,
it is because there is no light in them.
²¹And they shall pass through it,
hardly bestead and hungry:
and it shall come to pass, that when
they shall be hungry, they shall fret themselves,
and curse their king and their God,
and look upward.
²²And they shall look unto the earth;

and behold trouble and darkness,
dimness of anguish;
and they shall be driven to darkness.

9 Nevertheless the dimness shall not be such
as was in her vexation,
when at the first he lightly afflicted
the land of Zebulun and the land of Naphtali,
and afterward did more grievously afflict her
by the way of the sea,
beyond Jordan, in Galilee of the nations.
² The people that walked in darkness
have seen a great light:
they that dwell in the land
of the shadow of death,
upon them hath the light shined.
³ Thou hast multiplied the nation,
and not increased the joy;
they joy before thee
according to the joy in harvest,
and as men rejoice when they divide the spoil.
⁴ For thou hast broken the yoke of his burden,
and the staff of his shoulder,
the rod of his oppressor,
as in the day of Midian.

⁵ For every battle of the warrior is with
   confused noise, and garments rolled in blood;
      but this shall be with burning
   and fuel of fire.
⁶ For unto us a child is born, unto us a son is given;
   and the government shall be upon his shoulder;
      and his name shall be called
   Wonderful, Counsellor,
      The mighty God, The everlasting Father,
   The Prince of Peace.
⁷ Of the increase of his government and peace
   there shall be no end,
      upon the throne of David,
   and upon his kingdom,
      to order it, and to establish it
   with judgment and with justice
      from henceforth even for ever.
   The zeal of the Lord of hosts will perform this.
⁸ The Lord sent a word into Jacob,
   and it hath lighted upon Israel.
⁹ And all the people shall know,
   even Ephraim and the inhabitant of Samaria,
      that say in the pride and stoutness of heart,
¹⁰ 'The bricks are fallen down,
   but we will build with hewn stones;
      the sycomores are cut down,
   but we will change them into cedars.'
¹¹ Therefore the Lord shall set up

the adversaries of Rezin against him,
and join his enemies together;
¹² the Syrians before, and the Philistines behind;
and they shall devour Israel with open mouth.
For all this his anger is not turned away,
but his hand is stretched out still.
¹³ For the people turneth
not unto him that smiteth them,
neither do they seek the Lord of hosts.
¹⁴ Therefore the Lord will cut off from Israel
head and tail, branch and rush, in one day.
¹⁵ The ancient and honourable, he is the head;
and the prophet that teacheth lies, he is the tail.
¹⁶ For the leaders of this people cause them to err;
and they that are led of them are destroyed.
¹⁷ Therefore the Lord shall have no joy
in their young men,
neither shall have mercy
on their fatherless and widows,
for every one is an hypocrite and an evildoer,
and every mouth speaketh folly.
For all this his anger is not turned away,
but his hand is stretched out still.
¹⁸ For wickedness burneth as the fire:
it shall devour the briers and thorns,
and shall kindle in the thickets of the forest,
and they shall mount up
like the lifting up of smoke.

¹⁹ Through the wrath of the Lord of hosts
     is the land darkened,
          and the people shall be as the fuel of the fire:
     no man shall spare his brother.
²⁰ And he shall snatch on the right hand,
     and be hungry;
          and he shall eat on the left hand,
     and they shall not be satisfied;
          they shall eat every man
     the flesh of his own arm;
²¹ Manasseh, Ephraim; and Ephraim, Manasseh:
     and they together shall be against Judah.
          For all this his anger is not turned away,
     but his hand is stretched out still.

10   Woe unto them that decree unrighteous decrees,
          and that write grievousness
               which they have prescribed;
     ² to turn aside the needy from judgment,
          and to take away the right
     from the poor of my people,
          that widows may be their prey,
          and that they may rob the fatherless!
     ³ And what will ye do in the day of visitation,
          and in the desolation which shall come from far?

>   To whom will ye flee for help?
>   And where will ye leave your glory?
> ⁴ Without me they shall bow down
>   under the prisoners,
>   and they shall fall under the slain.
>   For all this his anger is not turned away,
>   but his hand is stretched out still.
> ⁵ O Assyrian, the rod of mine anger,
>   and the staff in their hand is mine indignation.
> ⁶ I will send him against an hypocritical nation,
>   and against the people of my wrath
>   will I give him a charge,
>   to take the spoil, and to take the prey,
>   and to tread them down
>   like the mire of the streets.
> ⁷ Howbeit he meaneth not so,
>   neither doth his heart think so;
>   but it is in his heart to destroy
>   and cut off nations not a few.
> ⁸ For he saith, 'Are not my princes altogether kings?
> ⁹ Is not Calno as Carchemish?
>   Is not Hamath as Arpad?
>   Is not Samaria as Damascus?
> ¹⁰ As my hand hath found the kingdoms of the idols,
>   and whose graven images did excel them
>   of Jerusalem and of Samaria,
> ¹¹ Shall I not, as I have done unto Samaria and her idols,
>   so do to Jerusalem and her idols?'

¹² Wherefore it shall come to pass,
that when the Lord hath performed
his whole work upon mount Zion
and on Jerusalem,
I will punish the fruit of the stout heart
of the king of Assyria,
and the glory of his high looks.
¹³ For he saith,
'By the strength of my hand I have done it,
and by my wisdom,
for I am prudent;
and I have removed the bounds of the people,
and have robbed their treasures,
and I have put down the inhabitants
like a valiant man.
¹⁴And my hand hath found as a nest
the riches of the people;
and as one gathereth eggs that are left,
have I gathered all the earth;
and there was none that moved the wing,
or opened the mouth, or peeped.'
¹⁵ Shall the axe boast itself against him
that heweth therewith?
Or shall the saw magnify itself
against him that shaketh it?
As if the rod should shake itself
against them that lift it up,
or as if the staff should lift up itself,
as if it were no wood.

¹⁶ Therefore shall the Lord, the Lord of hosts,
   send among his fat ones leanness;
      and under his glory he shall kindle a burning
   like the burning of a fire.
¹⁷And the light of Israel shall be for a fire,
   and his Holy One for a flame:
      and it shall burn and devour his thorns
   and his briers in one day.
¹⁸ and shall consume the glory of his forest,
   and of his fruitful field, both soul and body;
      and they shall be
   as when a standardbearer fainteth.
¹⁹And the rest of the trees of his forest shall be few,
   that a child may write them.
²⁰And it shall come to pass in that day,
   that the remnant of Israel,
      and such as are escaped of the house of Jacob,
   shall no more again stay upon
      him that smote them;
   but shall stay upon the Lord,
      the Holy One of Israel, in truth.
²¹The remnant shall return, even the remnant of Jacob,
   unto the mighty God.
²² For though thy people Israel
   be as the sand of the sea,
      yet a remnant of them shall return:
   the consumption decreed shall overflow
      with righteousness.

²³ For the Lord God of hosts shall make a consumption,
even determined, in the midst of all the land.
²⁴ Therefore thus saith the Lord God of hosts,
O my people that dwellest in Zion,
be not afraid of the Assyrian:
he shall smite thee with a rod,
and shall lift up his staff against thee
after the manner of Egypt.
²⁵ For yet a very little while,
and the indignation shall cease,
and mine anger in their destruction.
²⁶ And the Lord of hosts shall stir up a scourge
for him according to the slaughter of Midian
at the rock of Oreb:
and as his rod was upon the sea,
so shall he lift it up after the manner of Egypt.
²⁷ And it shall come to pass in that day,
that his burden shall be taken away
from off thy shoulder,
and his yoke from off thy neck,
and the yoke shall be destroyed
because of the anointing.
²⁸ He is come to Aiath, he is passed to Migron;
at Michmash he hath laid up his carriages;
²⁹ they are gone over the passage;
they have taken up their lodging at Geba;
Ramah is afraid;
Gibeah of Saul is fled.

³⁰ Lift up thy voice, O daughter of Gallim:
  cause it to be heard unto Laish,
    O poor Anathoth.
³¹ Madmenah is removed;
  the inhabitants of Gebim gather themselves to flee.
³² As yet shall he remain at Nob that day:
  he shall shake his hand
    against the mount of the daughter of Zion,
  the hill of Jerusalem.
³³ Behold, the Lord, the Lord of hosts,
  shall lop the bough with terror:
    and the high ones of stature
  shall be hewn down,
    and the haughty shall be humbled.
³⁴ And he shall cut down
  the thickets of the forest with iron,
    and Lebanon shall fall by a mighty one.

11 And there shall come forth a rod
  out of the stem of Jesse,
    and a Branch shall grow out of his roots.
² And the spirit of the Lord shall rest upon him,
  the spirit of wisdom and understanding,
    the spirit of counsel and might,
  the spirit of knowledge
    and of the fear of the Lord;

³ and shall make him of quick understanding
   in the fear of the Lord;
      and he shall not judge
      after the sight of his eyes,
         neither reprove after the hearing of his ears,
⁴ but with righteousness shall he judge the poor,
   and reprove with equity
      for the meek of the earth;
   and he shall smite the earth
      with the rod of his mouth,
   and with the breath of his lips
      shall he slay the wicked.
⁵ And righteousness shall be the girdle of his loins,
   and faithfulness the girdle of his reins.
⁶ The wolf also shall dwell with the lamb,
   and the leopard shall lie down with the kid;
      and the calf and the young lion
      and the fatling together;
         and a little child shall lead them.
⁷ And the cow and the bear shall feed;
   their young ones shall lie down together;
      and the lion shall eat straw like the ox.
⁸ And the sucking child shall play
   on the hole of the asp,
      and the weaned child shall put his hand
      on the cockatrice's den.
⁹ They shall not hurt nor destroy
   in all my holy mountain;

for the earth shall be full
of the knowledge of the Lord,
as the waters cover the sea.
[10]And in that day there shall be a root of Jesse,
which shall stand for an ensign of the people;
to it shall the Gentiles seek:
and his rest shall be glorious.
[11]And it shall come to pass in that day,
that the Lord shall set his hand again
the second time to recover
the remnant of his people, which shall be left,
from Assyria, and from Egypt,
and from Pathros, and from Cush, and from Elam,
and from Shinar, and from Hamath,
and from the islands of the sea.
[12]And he shall set up an ensign for the nations,
and shall assemble the outcasts of Israel,
and gather together the dispersed of Judah
from the four corners of the earth.
[13]The envy also of Ephraim shall depart,
and the adversaries of Judah shall be cut off:
Ephraim shall not envy Judah,
and Judah shall not vex Ephraim.
[14]But they shall fly upon the shoulders
of the Philistines toward the west;
they shall spoil them of the east together:
they shall lay their hand upon Edom and Moab;
and the children of Ammon shall obey them.

¹⁵And the Lord shall utterly destroy
the tongue of the Egyptian sea;
and with his mighty wind
shall he shake his hand over the river,
and shall smite it in the seven streams,
and make men go over dryshod.
¹⁶And there shall be an highway
for the remnant of his people,
which shall be left, from Assyria;
like as it was to Israel in the day
that he came up out of the land of Egypt.

12 And in that day thou shalt say,
O Lord, I will praise thee:
though thou wast angry with me,
thine anger is turned away,
and thou comfortedst me.
² Behold, God is my salvation;
I will trust, and not be afraid,
for the Lord Jehovah is my strength
and my song;
he also is become my salvation.
³ Therefore with joy shall ye draw water
out of the wells of salvation.
⁴And in that day shall ye say,

Praise the Lord, call upon his name,
 declare his doings among the people,
 make mention that his name is exalted.
⁵ Sing unto the Lord;
 for he hath done excellent things:
  this is known in all the earth.
⁶ Cry out and shout, thou inhabitant of Zion,
 for great is the Holy One of Israel
  in the midst of thee.

13 The burden of Babylon, which Isaiah
 the son of Amoz did see.
² Lift ye up a banner upon the high mountain,
 exalt the voice unto them, shake the hand,
  that they may go into the gates
 of the nobles.
³ I have commanded my sanctified ones,
 I have also called my mighty ones for mine anger,
  even them that rejoice in my highness.
⁴ The noise of a multitude in the mountains,
 like as of a great people;
  a tumultuous noise
 of the kingdoms of nations gathered together:
  the Lord of hosts mustereth
 the host of the battle.

⁵ They come from a far country,
    from the end of heaven, even the Lord,
        and the weapons of his indignation,
    to destroy the whole land.
⁶ Howl ye; for the day of the Lord is at hand;
    it shall come as a destruction from the Almighty.
⁷ Therefore shall all hands be faint,
    and every man's heart shall melt,
⁸ and they shall be afraid.
    Pangs and sorrows shall take hold of them;
        they shall be in pain
    as a woman that travaileth.
        They shall be amazed one at another;
    their faces shall be as flames.
⁹ Behold, the day of the Lord cometh,
    cruel both with wrath and fierce anger,
        to lay the land desolate:
    and he shall destroy the sinners thereof
        out of it.
¹⁰ For the stars of heaven and the constellations
    thereof shall not give their light:
        the sun shall be darkened in his going forth,
    and the moon shall not cause her light to shine.
¹¹ And I will punish the world for their evil,
    and the wicked for their iniquity;
        and I will cause the arrogancy
    of the proud to cease,
        and will lay low the haughtiness
    of the terrible.

¹² I will make a man more precious than fine gold;
  even a man than the golden wedge of Ophir.
¹³ Therefore I will shake the heavens,
  and the earth shall remove out of her place,
    in the wrath of the Lord of hosts,
  and in the day of his fierce anger.
¹⁴ And it shall be as the chased roe,
  and as a sheep that no man taketh up:
    they shall every man turn to his own people,
  and flee every one into his own land.
¹⁵ Every one that is found shall be thrust through;
  and every one that is joined unto them
    shall fall by the sword.
¹⁶ Their children also shall be dashed to pieces
  before their eyes;
    their houses shall be spoiled,
  and their wives ravished.
¹⁷ Behold, I will stir up the Medes against them,
  which shall not regard silver;
    and as for gold, they shall not delight in it.
¹⁸ Their bows also shall dash the young men to pieces;
  and they shall have no pity
  on the fruit of the womb;
    their eye shall not spare children.
¹⁹ And Babylon, the glory of kingdoms,
  the beauty of the Chaldees' excellency,
    shall be as when God overthrew
  Sodom and Gomorrah.

²⁰ It shall never be inhabited,
   neither shall it be dwelt in
      from generation to generation:
   neither shall the Arabian pitch tent there;
      neither shall the shepherds make their fold there.
²¹ But wild beasts of the desert shall lie there;
   and their houses shall be full of doleful creatures;
      and owls shall dwell there,
   and satyrs shall dance there.
²² And the wild beasts of the islands shall cry
   in their desolate houses,
      and dragons in their pleasant palaces:
   and her time is near to come,
      and her days shall not be prolonged.

14 For the Lord will have mercy on Jacob,
   and will yet choose Israel,
      and set them in their own land;
   and the strangers shall be joined with them,
      and they shall cleave to the house of Jacob.
² And the people shall take them,
   and bring them to their place;
      and the house of Israel shall possess them in
   the land of the Lord for servants and handmaids;
      and they shall take them captives,
   whose captives they were;

and they shall rule over their oppressors.
³And it shall come to pass in the day that the Lord
shall give thee rest from thy sorrow,
and from thy fear,
and from the hard bondage
wherein thou wast made to serve,
⁴that thou shalt take up this proverb
against the king of Babylon,
and say, How hath the oppressor ceased!
The golden city ceased!
⁵The Lord hath broken the staff of the wicked,
and the sceptre of the rulers.
⁶He who smote the people in wrath
with a continual stroke,
he that ruled the nations in anger,
is persecuted, and none hindereth.
⁷The whole earth is at rest, and is quiet:
they break forth into singing.
⁸Yea, the fir trees rejoice at thee,
and the cedars of Lebanon,
saying, 'Since thou art laid down,
no feller is come up against us.'
⁹Hell from beneath is moved for thee
to meet thee at thy coming;
it stirreth up the dead for thee,
even all the chief ones of the earth;
it hath raised up from their thrones
all the kings of the nations.

¹⁰All they shall speak and say unto thee,
'Art thou also become weak as we?
Art thou become like unto us?'
¹¹Thy pomp is brought down to the grave,
and the noise of thy viols:
the worm is spread under thee,
and the worms cover thee.
¹²How art thou fallen from heaven,
O Lucifer, son of the morning!
How art thou cut down to the ground,
which didst weaken the nations!
¹³For thou hast said in thine heart,
'I will ascend into heaven, I will exalt my throne
above the stars of God;
I will sit also upon the mount of the congregation,
in the sides of the north;
¹⁴I will ascend above the heights of the clouds;
I will be like the most High.'
¹⁵Yet thou shalt be brought down to hell,
to the sides of the pit.
¹⁶They that see thee shall narrowly look upon thee,
and consider thee, saying,
'Is this the man
that made the earth to tremble,
that did shake kingdoms;
¹⁷That made the world as a wilderness,
and destroyed the cities thereof;
that opened not the house of his prisoners?'

¹⁸All the kings of the nations,
even all of them, lie in glory,
every one in his own house.
¹⁹ But thou art cast out of thy grave
like an abominable branch,
and as the raiment of those that are slain,
thrust through with a sword,
that go down to the stones of the pit;
as a carcase trodden under feet.
²⁰ Thou shalt not be joined with them in burial,
because thou hast destroyed thy land,
and slain thy people:
the seed of evildoers shall never
be renowned.
²¹ Prepare slaughter for his children
for the iniquity of their fathers;
that they do not rise, nor possess the land,
nor fill the face of the world with cities.
²² For I will rise up against them,
saith the Lord of hosts,
and cut off from Babylon the name,
and remnant, and son, and nephew,
saith the Lord.
²³ I will also make it a possession for the bittern,
and pools of water:
and I will sweep it with the besom
of destruction,
saith the Lord of hosts.

²⁴ The Lord of hosts hath sworn, saying,
　　Surely as I have thought,
　　　　so shall it come to pass;
　　and as I have purposed, so shall it stand.
²⁵ that I will break the Assyrian in my land,
　　and upon my mountains tread him under foot;
　　　　then shall his yoke depart from off them,
　　and his burden depart from off their shoulders.
²⁶ This is the purpose that is purposed
　　upon the whole earth:
　　　　and this is the hand that is stretched out
　　upon all the nations.
²⁷ For the Lord of hosts hath purposed,
　　and who shall disannul it?
　　　　And his hand is stretched out,
　　and who shall turn it back?
²⁸ In the year that king Ahaz died was this burden.
²⁹ Rejoice not thou, whole Palestina,
　　because the rod of him that smote thee is broken,
　　　　for out of the serpent's root
　　shall come forth a cockatrice,
　　　　and his fruit shall be a fiery flying serpent.
³⁰ And the firstborn of the poor shall feed,
　　and the needy shall lie down in safety:
　　　　and I will kill thy root with famine,
　　and he shall slay thy remnant.
³¹ Howl, O gate; cry, O city;
　　thou, whole Palestina, art dissolved,

for there shall come from the north a smoke,
and none shall be alone in his appointed times.
³² What shall one then answer
the messengers of the nation?
That the Lord hath founded Zion,
and the poor of his people shall trust in it.

15 The burden of Moab. Because in the night
Ar of Moab is laid waste, and brought to silence;
because in the night
Kir of Moab is laid waste, and brought to silence,
² he is gone up to Bajith, and to Dibon,
the high places, to weep:
Moab shall howl over Nebo,
and over Medeba:
on all their heads shall be baldness,
and every beard cut off.
³ In their streets they shall gird themselves
with sackcloth:
on the tops of their houses, and in their streets,
every one shall howl, weeping abundantly.
⁴ And Heshbon shall cry, and Elealeh:
their voice shall be heard even unto Jahaz:
therefore the armed soldiers of Moab
shall cry out; his life shall be grievous unto him.

⁵ My heart shall cry out for Moab;
    his fugitives shall flee unto Zoar,
        an heifer of three years old;
    for by the mounting up of Luhith
        with weeping shall they go it up;
    for in the way of Horonaim they shall raise up
        a cry of destruction.
⁶ For the waters of Nimrim shall be desolate;
    for the hay is withered away, the grass faileth,
        there is no green thing.
⁷ Therefore the abundance they have gotten,
    and that which they have laid up,
        shall they carry away to the brook
    of the willows.
⁸ For the cry is gone round
    about the borders of Moab;
        the howling thereof unto Eglaim,
    and the howling thereof unto Beer-elim.
⁹ For the waters of Dimon shall be full of blood;
    for I will bring more upon Dimon,
        lions upon him that escapeth of Moab,
    and upon the remnant of the land.

16 Send ye the lamb to the ruler of the land
    from Sela to the wilderness,
        unto the mount of the daughter of Zion.
² For it shall be, that,

as a wandering bird
    cast out of the nest,
so the daughters of Moab
    shall be at the fords of Arnon.
³ Take counsel, execute judgment;
    make thy shadow as the night
        in the midst of the noonday; hide the outcasts;
    bewray not him that wandereth.
⁴ Let mine outcasts dwell with thee, Moab;
    be thou a covert to them
from the face of the spoiler;
    for the extortioner is at an end,
the spoiler ceaseth,
    the oppressors are consumed out of the land.
⁵ And in mercy shall the throne be established:
    and he shall sit upon it in truth
    in the tabernacle of David,
judging, and seeking judgment,
    and hasting righteousness.
⁶ We have heard of the pride of Moab,
    (he is very proud),
    even of his haughtiness, and his pride,
and his wrath;
    but his lies shall not be so.
⁷ Therefore shall Moab howl for Moab,
    every one shall howl;
    for the foundations of Kir-hareseth
shall ye mourn;
    surely they are stricken.

⁸For the fields of Heshbon languish,
and the vine of Sibmah.
The lords of the heathen have broken down
the principal plants thereof,
they are come even unto Jazer,
they wandered through the wilderness:
her branches are stretched out,
they are gone over the sea.
⁹Therefore I will bewail with the weeping of Jazer
the vine of Sibmah.
I will water thee with my tears,
O Heshbon, and Elealeh;
for the shouting for thy summer fruits
and for thy harvest is fallen.
¹⁰And gladness is taken away,
and joy out of the plentiful field;
and in the vineyards there shall be no singing,
neither shall there be shouting;
the treaders shall tread out no wine
in their presses;
I have made their vintage shouting to cease.
¹¹Wherefore my bowels shall sound like
an harp for Moab,
and mine inward parts for Kir-haresh.
¹²And it shall come to pass, when it is seen that Moab
is weary on the high place,
that he shall come to his sanctuary to pray;
but he shall not prevail.

¹³ This is the word that the Lord hath spoken
    concerning Moab since that time.
¹⁴ But now the Lord hath spoken, saying,
    Within three years, as the years of an hireling,
        and the glory of Moab shall be contemned,
    with all that great multitude;
        and the remnant shall be very small and feeble.

17

The burden of Damascus. Behold,
    Damascus is taken away from being a city,
        and it shall be a ruinous heap.
² The cities of Aroer are forsaken:
    they shall be for flocks, which shall lie down,
        and none shall make them afraid.
³ The fortress also shall cease from Ephraim,
    and the kingdom from Damascus,
        and the remnant of Syria:
    they shall be as the glory of the children of Israel,
        saith the Lord of hosts.
⁴ And in that day it shall come to pass,
    that the glory of Jacob shall be made thin,
        and the fatness of his flesh shall wax lean.
⁵ And it shall be as when
    the harvestman gathereth the corn,
        and reapeth the ears with his arm;
    and it shall be as he that gathereth ears
        in the valley of Rephaim.

⁶ Yet gleaning grapes shall be left in it,
  as the shaking of an olive tree,
    two or three berries in the top of
  the uppermost bough,
    four or five in the outmost
  fruitful branches thereof,
    saith the Lord God of Israel.
⁷ At that day shall a man look to his Maker,
  and his eyes shall have respect
    to the Holy One of Israel.
⁸ And he shall not look to the altars,
  the work of his hands,
    neither shall respect that
  which his fingers have made,
    either the groves, or the images.
⁹ In that day shall his strong cities be
  as a forsaken bough,
    and an uppermost branch,
  which they left because of the children of Israel,
    and there shall be desolation.
¹⁰ Because thou hast forgotten
  the God of thy salvation,
    and hast not been mindful
  of the rock of thy strength,
    therefore shalt thou plant pleasant plants,
  and shalt set it with strange slips.
¹¹ In the day shalt thou make thy plant to grow,
  and in the morning
    shalt thou make thy seed to flourish,

but the harvest shall be a heap in the day
of grief and of desperate sorrow.
¹² Woe to the multitude of many people,
which make a noise like the noise of the seas;
and to the rushing of nations,
that make a rushing
like the rushing of mighty waters!
¹³ The nations shall rush
like the rushing of many waters,
but God shall rebuke them,
and they shall flee far off, and shall be chased
as the chaff of the mountains before the wind,
and like a rolling thing before the whirlwind.
¹⁴ And behold at eveningtide trouble;
and before the morning he is not.
This is the portion of them that spoil us,
and the lot of them that rob us.

18 Woe to the land shadowing with wings,
which is beyond the rivers of Ethiopia,
² that sendeth ambassadors by the sea,
even in vessels of bulrushes upon the waters,
saying, Go, ye swift messengers,
to a nation scattered and peeled, to a people
terrible from their beginning hitherto;
a nation meted out and trodden down,
whose land the rivers have spoiled!

³All ye inhabitants of the world,
>and dwellers on the earth,
>>see ye, when he lifteth up an ensign
>on the mountains;
>>and when he bloweth a trumpet, hear ye.
⁴For so the Lord said unto me,
>I will take my rest, and I will consider in my
>>dwelling place
>like a clear heat upon herbs,
>>and like a cloud of dew in the heat of harvest.
⁵For afore the harvest, when the bud is perfect,
>and the sour grape is ripening in the flower,
>>he shall both cut off the sprigs
>with pruning hooks,
>>and take away and cut down the branches.
⁶They shall be left together
>unto the fowls of the mountains,
>>and to the beasts of the earth,
>and the fowls shall summer upon them,
>>and all the beasts of the earth
>shall winter upon them.
⁷In that time shall the present
>be brought unto the Lord of hosts
>>of a people scattered and peeled,
>and from a people terrible
>>from their beginning hitherto;
>>a nation meted out and trodden under foot,
>>>whose land the rivers have spoiled,

to the place of the name of the Lord of hosts,
    the mount Zion.

19 The burden of Egypt. Behold, the Lord rideth
    upon a swift cloud, and shall come into Egypt;
        and the idols of Egypt shall be moved
    at his presence,
        and the heart of Egypt shall melt
    in the midst of it.
²And I will set the Egyptians against the Egyptians,
    and they shall fight every one against his brother,
        and every one against his neighbour;
    city against city, and kingdom against kingdom.
³And the spirit of Egypt shall fail
    in the midst thereof;
        and I will destroy the counsel thereof;
    and they shall seek to the idols,
        and to the charmers,
    and to them that have familiar spirits,
        and to the wizards.
⁴And the Egyptians will I give over
    into the hand of a cruel lord;
        and a fierce king shall rule over them,
    saith the Lord, the Lord of hosts.
⁵And the waters shall fail from the sea,
    and the river shall be wasted and dried up.

⁶And they shall turn the rivers far away;
  and the brooks of defence shall be emptied
    and dried up:
  the reeds and flags shall wither.
⁷The paper reeds by the brooks,
  by the mouth of the brooks,
    and every thing sown by the brooks,
  shall wither, be driven away, and be no more.
⁸The fishers also shall mourn,
  and all they that cast angle into the brooks
    shall lament,
  and they that spread nets upon the waters
    shall languish.
⁹Moreover they that work in fine flax,
  and they that weave networks,
    shall be confounded.
¹⁰And they shall be broken in the purposes thereof,
  all that make sluices and ponds for fish.
¹¹Surely the princes of Zoan are fools,
  the counsel of the wise counsellors of Pharaoh
    is become brutish.
  How say ye unto Pharaoh,
    'I am the son of the wise,
  the son of ancient kings'?
¹²Where are they? Where are thy wise men?
  And let them tell thee now,
    and let them know what the Lord of hosts
  hath purposed upon Egypt.

¹³ The princes of Zoan are become fools,
  the princes of Noph are deceived;
    they have also seduced Egypt,
  even they that are the stay of the tribes thereof.
¹⁴ The Lord hath mingled a perverse spirit
  in the midst thereof;
    and they have caused Egypt to err in
  every work thereof,
    as a drunken man staggereth in his vomit.
¹⁵ Neither shall there be any work for Egypt,
  which the head or tail, branch or rush, may do.
¹⁶ In that day shall Egypt be like unto women;
  and it shall be afraid and fear because of
    the shaking of the hand of the Lord of hosts,
  which he shaketh over it.
¹⁷ And the land of Judah shall be a terror unto Egypt,
  every one that maketh mention thereof
    shall be afraid in himself,
  because of the counsel of the Lord of hosts,
    which he hath determined against it.
¹⁸ In that day shall five cities in the land of Egypt
  speak the language of Canaan,
    and swear to the Lord of hosts;
  one shall be called, 'The city of destruction'.
¹⁹ In that day shall there be an altar to the Lord
  in the midst of the land of Egypt,
    and a pillar at the border thereof to
  the Lord.

²⁰And it shall be for a sign and for a witness
  unto the Lord of hosts in the land of Egypt
   for they shall cry unto the Lord
  because of the oppressors,
   and he shall send them a saviour,
  and a great one, and he shall deliver them.
²¹And the Lord shall be known to Egypt,
  and the Egyptians shall know the Lord
   in that day,
  and shall do sacrifice and oblation;
   yea, they shall vow a vow unto the Lord,
  and perform it.
²²And the Lord shall smite Egypt;
  he shall smite and heal it;
   and they shall return even to the Lord,
  and he shall be intreated of them,
   and shall heal them.
²³In that day shall there be a highway
  out of Egypt to Assyria,
   and the Assyrian shall come into Egypt,
  and the Egyptian into Assyria,
   and the Egyptians shall serve
  with the Assyrians.
²⁴In that day shall Israel be the third
  with Egypt and with Assyria,
   even a blessing in the midst of the land,
²⁵whom the Lord of hosts shall bless, saying,
  'Blessed be Egypt my people,

and Assyria the work of my hands,
and Israel mine inheritance.'

20 In the year that Tartan came unto Ashdod
(when Sargon the king of Assyria sent him),
and fought against Ashdod,
and took it;
²at the same time spake the Lord by Isaiah
the son of Amoz, saying,
'Go and loose the sackcloth from off thy loins,
and put off thy shoe from thy foot.'
And he did so, walking naked and barefoot.
³And the Lord said, 'Like as my servant Isaiah
hath walked naked and barefoot three years
for a sign and wonder upon Egypt
and upon Ethiopia;
⁴so shall the king of Assyria lead away
the Egyptians prisoners,
and the Ethiopians captives, young and old,
naked and barefoot,
even with their buttocks uncovered,
to the shame of Egypt.
⁵And they shall be afraid and ashamed
of Ethiopia their expectation,
and of Egypt their glory.

⁶And the inhabitant of this isle shall say in that day,
"Behold, such is our expectation,
whither we flee for help to be delivered
from the king of Assyria:
and how shall we escape?"'

21 The burden of the desert of the sea.
As whirlwinds in the south pass through;
so it cometh from the desert,
from a terrible land.
²A grievous vision is declared unto me;
the treacherous dealer dealeth treacherously,
and the spoiler spoileth.
Go up, O Elam; besiege, O Media;
all the sighing thereof have I made to cease.
³Therefore are my loins filled with pain;
pangs have taken hold upon me,
as the pangs of a woman that travaileth;
I was bowed down at the hearing of it;
I was dismayed at the seeing of it.
⁴My heart panted, fearfulness affrighted me:
the night of my pleasure hath he turned
into fear unto me.
⁵Prepare the table, watch in the watch-tower,
eat, drink:
arise, ye princes, and anoint the shield.

⁶ For thus hath the Lord said unto me,
  'Go, set a watchman,
    let him declare what he seeth.'
⁷ And he saw a chariot with a couple of horsemen,
    a chariot of asses, and a chariot of camels;
      and he hearkened diligently with much heed.
⁸ And he cried, 'A lion; my lord,
    I stand continually upon the watchtower
      in the daytime,
    and I am set in my ward whole nights;
⁹ and, behold, here cometh a chariot of men,
    with a couple of horsemen.'
      And he answered and said,
      'Babylon is fallen, is fallen;
        and all the graven images of her gods
      he hath broken unto the ground.'
¹⁰ O my threshing, and the corn of my floor:
    that which I have heard of
      the Lord of hosts, the God of Israel,
    have I declared unto you.
¹¹ The burden of Dumah. He calleth to me out of Seir,
    'Watchman, what of the night?
      Watchman, what of the night?'
¹² The watchman said,
    'The morning cometh, and also the night:
      if ye will enquire, enquire ye; return, come.'
¹³ The burden upon Arabia.
    In the forest in Arabia shall ye lodge,
      O ye travelling companies of Dedanim.

¹⁴ The inhabitants of the land of Tema
    brought water to him that was thirsty,
        they prevented with their bread him that fled.
¹⁵ For they fled from the swords,
    from the drawn sword,
        and from the bent bow,
    and from the grievousness of war.
¹⁶ For thus hath the Lord said unto me,
    'Within a year, according to the years
        of an hireling,
    and all the glory of Kedar shall fail;
¹⁷and the residue of the number of archers,
    the mighty men of the children of Kedar,
        shall be diminished;
    for the Lord God of Israel hath spoken it.

22 The burden of the valley of vision.
    What aileth thee now,
        that thou art wholly gone up
    to the house-tops?
² Thou that art full of stirs, a tumultuous city,
    a joyous city:
        thy slain men are not slain with the sword,
    nor dead in battle.
³All thy rulers are fled together,
    they are bound by the archers:

all that are found in thee are bound together,
which have fled from far.
⁴ Therefore said I, Look away from me;
I will weep bitterly, labour not to comfort me,
because of the spoiling of the daughter
of my people.
⁵ For it is a day of trouble, and of treading down,
and of perplexity by the Lord God of hosts
in the valley of vision,
breaking down the walls,
and of crying to the mountains.
⁶ And Elam bare the quiver with chariots
of men and horsemen,
and Kir uncovered the shield.
⁷ And it shall come to pass,
that thy choicest valleys shall be full of chariots,
and the horsemen shall set themselves
in array at the gate.
⁸ And he discovered the covering of Judah,
and thou didst look in that day to the armour
of the house of the forest.
⁹ Ye have seen also the breaches of the city of David,
that they are many;
and ye gathered together the waters
of the lower pool.
¹⁰ And ye have numbered the houses of Jerusalem,
and the houses have ye broken down
to fortify the wall.

¹¹ Ye made also a ditch between the two walls
for the water of the old pool,
but ye have not looked
unto the maker thereof,
neither had respect unto him
that fashioned it long ago.
¹² And in that day did the Lord God of hosts
call to weeping, and to mourning,
and to baldness,
and to girding with sack-cloth.
¹³ And behold joy and gladness,
slaying oxen, and killing sheep,
eating flesh, and drinking wine:
let us eat and drink; for to morrow we shall die.
¹⁴ And it was revealed in mine ears
by the Lord of hosts,
Surely this iniquity shall not be purged
from you till ye die, saith the Lord God of hosts.
¹⁵ Thus saith the Lord God of hosts,
Go, get thee unto this treasurer,
even unto Shebna,
which is over the house, and say,
¹⁶ What hast thou here?
And whom hast thou here,
that thou hast hewed thee
out a sepulchre here,
as he that heweth him out
a sepulchre on high,

and that graveth an habitation
for himself in a rock?
¹⁷ Behold, the Lord will carry thee away
with a mighty captivity,
and will surely cover thee.
¹⁸ He will surely violently turn and toss thee
like a ball into a large country:
there shalt thou die, and there the chariots of
thy glory shall be the shame of
thy lord's house.
¹⁹ And I will drive thee from thy station,
and from thy state shall he pull thee down.
²⁰ And it shall come to pass in that day,
that I will call my servant Eliakim
the son of Hilkiah,
²¹ and I will clothe him with thy robe,
and strengthen him with thy girdle,
and I will commit thy government
into his hand, and he shall be a father
to the inhabitants of Jerusalem,
and to the house of Judah.
²² And the key of the house of David
will I lay upon his shoulder;
so he shall open, and none shall shut;
and he shall shut, and none shall open.
²³ And I will fasten him as a nail in a sure place;
and he shall be for a glorious throne
to his father's house.

²⁴And they shall hang upon him
all the glory of his father's house,
the offspring and the issue,
all vessels of small quantity,
from the vessels of cups,
even to all the vessels of flagons.
²⁵ In that day, saith the Lord of hosts,
shall the nail that is fastened in the sure place
be removed, and be cut down, and fall;
and the burden that was upon it
shall be cut off,
for the Lord hath spoken it.

23 The burden of Tyre.
Howl, ye ships of Tarshish; for it is laid waste,
so that there is no house, no entering in:
from the land of Chittim it is revealed to them.
² Be still, ye inhabitants of the isle;
thou whom the merchants of Zidon,
that pass over the sea, have replenished.
³And by great waters the seed of Sihor,
the harvest of the river, is her revenue;
and she is a mart of nations.
⁴ Be thou ashamed, O Zidon; for the sea hath spoken,
even the strength of the sea, saying,

'I travail not, nor bring forth children,
  neither do I nourish up young men,
    nor bring up virgins.'
⁵As at the report concerning Egypt,
  so shall they be sorely pained
    at the report of Tyre.
⁶ Pass ye over to Tarshish;
  howl, ye inhabitants of the isle.
⁷ Is this your joyous city,
  whose antiquity is of ancient days?
    Her own feet shall carry her
  afar off to sojourn.
⁸ Who hath taken this counsel against Tyre,
  the crowning city, whose merchants are princes,
    whose traffickers are the honourable
  of the earth?
⁹ The Lord of hosts hath purposed it,
  to stain the pride of all glory,
    and to bring into contempt
  all the honourable of the earth.
¹⁰ Pass through thy land as a river,
  O daughter of Tarshish:
    there is no more strength.
¹¹ He stretched out his hand over the sea,
  he shook the kingdoms;
    the Lord hath given a commandment
  against the merchant city,
    to destroy the strongholds thereof.

¹²And he said, 'Thou shalt no more rejoice,
    O thou oppressed virgin, daughter of Zidon:
        arise, pass over to Chittim;
    there also shalt thou have no rest.'
¹³ Behold the land of the Chaldeans;
    this people was not, till the Assyrian founded it
        for them that dwell in the wilderness:
    they set up the towers thereof,
        they raised up the palaces thereof;
    and he brought it to ruin.
¹⁴ Howl, ye ships of Tarshish,
    for your strength is laid waste.
¹⁵And it shall come to pass in that day,
    that Tyre shall be forgotten seventy years,
        according to the days of one king:
    after the end of seventy years shall Tyre sing
        as an harlot.
¹⁶ Take an harp, go about the city,
    thou harlot that hast been forgotten;
        make sweet melody, sing many songs,
    that thou mayest be remembered.
¹⁷And it shall come to pass
    after the end of seventy years,
        that the Lord will visit Tyre,
    and she shall turn to her hire,
        and shall commit fornication
    with all the kingdoms of the world
        upon the face of the earth.

[18]And her merchandise and her hire
   shall be holiness to the Lord.
      It shall not be treasured nor laid up;
      for her merchandise shall be for them that dwell
         before the Lord,
   to eat sufficiently, and for durable clothing.

24 Behold, the Lord maketh the earth empty,
      and maketh it waste, and turneth it upside down,
         and scattereth abroad
      the inhabitants thereof.
   [2]And it shall be, as with the people,
      so with the priest;
         as with the servant, so with his master;
      as with the maid, so with her mistress;
         as with the buyer, so with the seller;
      as with the lender, so with the borrower;
         as with the taker of usury,
      so with the giver of usury to him.
   [3]The land shall be utterly emptied,
      and utterly spoiled,
         for the Lord hath spoken this word.
   [4]The earth mourneth and fadeth away,
      the world languisheth and fadeth away,
         the haughty people of the earth do languish.

⁵ The earth also is defiled
    under the inhabitants thereof;
        because they have transgressed the laws,
    changed the ordinance,
        broken the everlasting covenant.
⁶ Therefore hath the curse devoured the earth,
    and they that dwell therein are desolate;
        therefore the inhabitants
    of the earth are burned, and few men left.
⁷ The new wine mourneth, the vine languisheth,
    all the merryhearted do sigh.
⁸ The mirth of tabrets ceaseth,
    the noise of them that rejoice endeth,
        the joy of the harp ceaseth.
⁹ They shall not drink wine with a song;
    strong drink shall be bitter to them that drink it.
¹⁰ The city of confusion is broken down;
    every house is shut up,
        that no man may come in.
¹¹ There is a crying for wine in the streets;
    all joy is darkened,
        the mirth of the land is gone.
¹² In the city is left desolation,
    and the gate is smitten with destruction.
¹³ When thus it shall be in the midst of the land
    among the people,
        there shall be as the shaking of an olive tree,
    and as the gleaning grapes

when the vintage is done.

¹⁴ They shall lift up their voice,
    they shall sing for the majesty of the Lord,
        they shall cry aloud from the sea.

¹⁵ Wherefore glorify ye the Lord in the fires,
    even the name of the Lord God of Israel
        in the isles of the sea.

¹⁶ From the uttermost part of the earth
    have we heard songs, even glory to the righteous.
        But I said,
    My leanness, my leanness, woe unto me!
        The treacherous dealers have dealt
    treacherously;
        yea, the treacherous dealers
    have dealt very treacherously.

¹⁷ Fear, and the pit, and the snare,
    are upon thee, O inhabitant of the earth.

¹⁸ And it shall come to pass,
    that he who fleeth from the noise of the fear
        shall fall into the pit;
    and he that cometh up out of the midst of the pit
        shall be taken in the snare;
    for the windows from on high are open,
        and the foundations of the earth
    do shake.

¹⁹ The earth is utterly broken down,
    the earth is clean dissolved,
        the earth is moved exceedingly.

²⁰ The earth shall reel to and fro like a drunkard,
and shall be removed like a cottage;
and the transgression thereof
shall be heavy upon it;
and it shall fall, and not rise again.
²¹And it shall come to pass in that day,
that the Lord shall punish the host
of the high ones that are on high,
and the kings of the earth upon the earth.
²²And they shall be gathered together,
as prisoners are gathered in the pit,
and shall be shut up in the prison,
and after many days shall they be visited.
²³ Then the moon shall be confounded,
and the sun ashamed,
when the Lord of hosts shall reign
in mount Zion, and in Jerusalem,
and before his ancients gloriously.

25

Lord, thou art my God;
I will exalt thee, I will praise thy name;
for thou hast done wonderful things;
thy counsels of old are faithfulness
and truth.
² For thou hast made of a city an heap;
of a defenced city a ruin:

a palace of strangers to be no city;
it shall never be built.

3 Therefore shall the strong people glorify thee,
the city of the terrible nations shall fear thee.

4 For thou hast been a strength to the poor,
a strength to the needy in his distress,
a refuge from the storm,
a shadow from the heat,
when the blast of the terrible ones
is as a storm against the wall.

5 Thou shalt bring down the noise of strangers,
as the heat in a dry place;
even the heat with the shadow of a cloud;
the branch of the terrible ones
shall be brought low.

6 And in this mountain shall the Lord of hosts
make unto all people a feast of fat things,
a feast of wines on the lees,
of fat things full of marrow,
of wines on the lees well refined.

7 And he will destroy in this mountain
the face of the covering cast over all people,
and the vail that is spread over all nations.

8 He will swallow up death in victory;
and the Lord God will wipe away tears
from off all faces;
and the rebuke of his people
shall he take away from off all the earth;
for the Lord hath spoken it.

⁹And it shall be said in that day, Lo, this is our God;
we have waited for him, and he will save us:
this is the Lord; we have waited for him,
we will be glad and rejoice in his salvation.
¹⁰For in this mountain shall the hand of the Lord rest,
and Moab shall be trodden down under him,
even as straw is trodden down
for the dunghill.
¹¹And he shall spread forth his hands
in the midst of them,
as he that swimmeth spreadeth forth
his hands to swim;
and he shall bring down their pride
together with the spoils of their hands.
¹²And the fortress of the high fort of thy walls
shall he bring down, lay low,
and bring to the ground, even to the dust.

26 In that day shall this song be sung
in the land of Judah:
We have a strong city;
salvation will God appoint
for walls and bulwarks.
²Open ye the gates,
that the righteous nation
which keepeth the truth may enter in.
³Thou wilt keep him in perfect peace,

whose mind is stayed on thee,
　　because he trusteth in thee.
⁴ Trust ye in the Lord for ever,
　　for in the Lord Jehovah is everlasting strength.
⁵ For he bringeth down them that dwell on high;
　　the lofty city, he layeth it low;
　　　　he layeth it low, even to the ground;
　　he bringeth it even to the dust.
⁶ The foot shall tread it down,
　　even the feet of the poor,
　　　　and the steps of the needy.
⁷ The way of the just is uprightness:
　　thou, most upright,
　　　　dost weigh the path of the just.
⁸ Yea, in the way of thy judgments, O Lord,
　　have we waited for thee;
　　　　the desire of our soul is to thy name,
　　and to the remembrance of thee.
⁹ With my soul have I desired thee in the night;
　　yea, with my spirit within me
　　　　will I seek thee early;
　　for when thy judgments are in the earth,
　　　　the inhabitants of the world
　　will learn righteousness.
¹⁰ Let favour be shewed to the wicked,
　　yet will he not learn righteousness:
　　　　in the land of uprightness
　　will he deal unjustly,
　　　　and will not behold the majesty of the Lord.

¹¹ Lord, when thy hand is lifted up, they will not see:
but they shall see, and be ashamed
for their envy at the people;
yea, the fire of thine enemies shall devour them.
¹² Lord, thou wilt ordain peace for us
for thou also hast wrought all our works in us.
¹³ O Lord our God, other lords beside thee
have had dominion over us,
but by thee only will we make mention
of thy name.
¹⁴ They are dead, they shall not live;
they are deceased, they shall not rise;
therefore hast thou visited
and destroyed them,
and made all their memory to perish.
¹⁵ Thou hast increased the nation, O Lord,
thou hast increased the nation; thou art glorified;
thou hadst removed it far unto
all the ends of the earth.
¹⁶ Lord, in trouble have they visited thee,
they poured out a prayer
when thy chastening was upon them.
¹⁷ Like as a woman with child,
that draweth near the time of her delivery,
is in pain, and crieth out in her pangs;
so have we been in thy sight, O Lord.
¹⁸ We have been with child, we have been in pain,
we have as it were brought forth wind;

we have not wrought
any deliverance in the earth;
neither have the inhabitants
of the world fallen.
¹⁹ Thy dead men shall live,
together with my dead body shall they arise.
Awake and sing, ye that dwell in dust,
for thy dew is as the dew of herbs,
and the earth shall cast out the dead.
²⁰ Come, my people, enter thou into thy chambers,
and shut thy doors about thee:
hide thyself as it were for a little moment,
until the indignation be overpast.
²¹ For, behold, the Lord cometh out of his place
to punish the inhabitants of the earth
for their iniquity:
the earth also shall disclose her blood,
and shall no more cover her slain.

27 In that day the Lord with his sore
and great and strong sword
shall punish leviathan the piercing serpent,
even leviathan that crooked serpent;
and he shall slay the dragon that is in the sea.
² In that day sing ye unto her, a vineyard of red wine.
³ I the Lord do keep it; I will water it every moment:
lest any hurt it, I will keep it night and day.

⁴ Fury is not in me: who would set the briers
and thorns against me in battle?
I would go through them,
I would burn them together.
⁵ Or let him take hold of my strength,
that he may make peace with me;
and he shall make peace with me.
⁶ He shall cause them that come of Jacob to take root:
Israel shall blossom and bud,
and fill the face of the world with fruit.
⁷ Hath he smitten him,
as he smote those that smote him?
Or is he slain according to the slaughter of
them that are slain by him?
⁸ In measure, when it shooteth forth,
thou wilt debate with it:
he stayeth his rough wind in the day
of the east wind.
⁹ By this therefore shall the iniquity
of Jacob be purged;
and this is all the fruit to take away his sin;
when he maketh all the stones of the altar as
chalkstones that are beaten in sunder,
the groves and images shall not stand up.
¹⁰ Yet the defenced city shall be desolate,
and the habitation forsaken,
and left like a wilderness:
there shall the calf feed,

and there shall he lie down,
and consume the branches thereof.
11 When the boughs thereof are withered,
they shall be broken off;
the women come, and set them on fire,
for it is a people of no understanding;
therefore he that made them
will not have mercy on them,
and he that formed them
will shew them no favour.
12 And it shall come to pass in that day,
that the Lord shall beat off from the channel
of the river unto the stream of Egypt,
and ye shall be gathered one by one,
O ye children of Israel.
13 And it shall come to pass in that day,
that the great trumpet shall be blown,
and they shall come which were ready
to perish in the land of Assyria,
and the outcasts in the land of Egypt,
and shall worship the Lord
in the holy mount at Jerusalem.

28 Woe to the crown of pride,
to the drunkards of Ephraim,
whose glorious beauty is a fading flower,
which are on the head of the fat valleys
of them that are overcome with wine!

² Behold, the Lord hath a mighty and strong one,
    which as a tempest of hail
      and a destroying storm,
    as a flood of mighty waters overflowing,
      shall cast down to the earth
    with the hand.
³ The crown of pride, the drunkards of Ephraim,
    shall be trodden under feet.
⁴ And the glorious beauty,
    which is on the head of the fat valley,
      shall be a fading flower,
    and as the hasty fruit before the summer;
      which when he that looketh upon it seeth,
    while it is yet in his hand he eateth it up.
⁵ In that day shall the Lord of hosts be
    for a crown of glory,
      and for a diadem of beauty,
    unto the residue of his people,
⁶ and for a spirit of judgment to him
    that sitteth in judgment,
      and for strength to them
    that turn the battle to the gate.
⁷ But they also have erred through wine,
    and through strong drink are out of the way;
      the priest and the prophet have erred
    through strong drink,
      they are swallowed up of wine,
    they are out of the way through strong drink;

they err in vision,
  they stumble in judgment.
⁸ For all tables are full of vomit and filthiness,
  so that there is no place clean.
⁹ Whom shall he teach knowledge?
  And whom shall he make
    to understand doctrine?
  Them that are weaned from the milk,
    and drawn from the breasts.
¹⁰ For precept must be upon precept,
  precept upon precept;
    line upon line, line upon line;
  here a little, and there a little.
¹¹ For with stammering lips and another tongue
  will he speak to this people.
¹² To whom he said,
  'This is the rest wherewith ye may cause
    the weary to rest; and this is the refreshing':
  yet they would not hear.
¹³ But the word of the Lord was unto them
  precept upon precept, precept upon precept;
    line upon line, line upon line;
  here a little, and there a little;
    that they might go, and fall backward,
  and be broken, and snared, and taken.
¹⁴ Wherefore hear the word of the Lord,
  ye scornful men, that rule this people
    which is in Jerusalem.

¹⁵ Because ye have said,

    'We have made a covenant with death,

    and with hell are we at agreement;

        when the overflowing scourge

    shall pass through,

        it shall not come unto us:

    for we have made lies our refuge,

        and under falsehood have we hid ourselves'.

¹⁶ Therefore thus saith the Lord God,

    Behold, I lay in Zion for a foundation a stone,

        a tried stone, a precious corner stone,

    a sure foundation:

        he that believeth shall not make haste.

¹⁷ Judgment also will I lay to the line,

    and righteousness to the plummet;

        and the hail shall sweep away

    the refuge of lies,

        and the waters shall overflow the hiding place.

¹⁸ And your covenant with death shall be disannulled,

    and your agreement with hell shall not stand;

        when the overflowing scourge

    shall pass through,

        then ye shall be trodden down by it.

¹⁹ From the time that it goeth forth it shall take you,

    for morning by morning shall it pass over,

        by day and by night;

    and it shall be a vexation

only to understand the report.

²⁰ For the bed is shorter than
that a man can stretch himself on it,
and the covering narrower than
that he can wrap himself in it.

²¹ For the Lord shall rise up as in mount Perazim,
he shall be wroth as in the valley of Gibeon,
that he may do his work, his strange work;
and bring to pass his act, his strange act.

²² Now therefore be ye not mockers,
lest your bands be made strong,
for I have heard from the Lord God of hosts
a consumption,
even determined upon the whole earth.

²³ Give ye ear, and hear my voice;
hearken, and hear my speech.

²⁴ Doth the plowman plow all day to sow?
Doth he open and break the clods
of his ground?

²⁵ When he hath made plain the face thereof,
doth he not cast abroad the fitches,
and scatter the cummin,
and cast in the principal wheat
and the appointed barley
and the rie in their place?

²⁶ For his God doth instruct him to discretion,
and doth teach him.

²⁷ For the fitches are not threshed
    with a threshing instrument,
        neither is a cart wheel turned about
    upon the cummin;
        but the fitches are beaten out with a staff,
    and the cummin with a rod.
²⁸ Bread corn is bruised;
    because he will not ever be threshing it,
        nor break it with the wheel of his cart,
    nor bruise it with his horsemen.
²⁹ This also cometh forth from the Lord of hosts,
    which is wonderful in counsel,
        and excellent in working.

29 Woe to Ariel, to Ariel, the city where David dwelt!
    Add ye year to year; let them kill sacrifices.
² Yet I will distress Ariel, and there shall be heaviness
    and sorrow,
        and it shall be unto me as Ariel.
³ And I will camp against thee round about,
    and will lay siege against thee with a mount,
        and I will raise forts against thee.
⁴ And thou shalt be brought down,
    and shalt speak out of the ground,
        and thy speech shall be low out of the dust,

and thy voice shall be,
    as of one that hath a familiar spirit,
out of the ground,
    and thy speech shall whisper
out of the dust.
⁵ Moreover the multitude of thy strangers
    shall be like small dust,
        and the multitude of the terrible ones
    shall be as chaff that passeth away:
        yea, it shall be at an instant suddenly.
⁶ Thou shalt be visited of the Lord of hosts
    with thunder, and with earthquake,
        and great noise, with storm and tempest,
    and the flame of devouring fire.
⁷ And the multitude of all the nations
    that fight against Ariel,
        even all that fight against her
    and her munition, and that distress her,
        shall be as a dream of a night vision.
⁸ It shall even be as when an hungry man dreameth,
    and, behold, he eateth;
        but he awaketh, and his soul is empty:
    or as when a thirsty man dreameth,
        and, behold, he drinketh;
    but he awaketh, and, behold, he is faint,
        and his soul hath appetite:
    so shall the multitude of all the nations be,
        that fight against mount Zion.

⁹ Stay yourselves, and wonder;
   cry ye out, and cry: they are drunken,
      but not with wine;
   they stagger, but not with strong drink.
¹⁰ For the Lord hath poured out upon you the spirit of
   deep sleep, and hath closed your eyes:
      the prophets and your rulers,
   the seers hath he covered.
¹¹ And the vision of all is become unto you
   as the words of a book that is sealed,
      which men deliver to one that is learned,
   saying, 'Read this, I pray thee':
      and he saith, 'I cannot; for it is sealed.'
¹² And the book is delivered to him that is not
   learned, saying, 'Read this, I pray thee':
      and he saith, 'I am not learned.'
¹³ Wherefore the Lord said,
   Forasmuch as this people draw near me
      with their mouth,
   and with their lips do honour me,
      but have removed their heart far from me,
   and their fear toward me is taught
      by the precept of men;
¹⁴ therefore, behold, I will proceed to do
   a marvellous work among this people,
      even a marvellous work and a wonder,
   for the wisdom of their wise men shall perish,
      and the understanding of their prudent men

shall be hid.
¹⁵ Woe unto them that seek deep to hide
their counsel from the Lord,
and their works are in the dark, and they say,
'Who seeth us? And who knoweth us?'
¹⁶ Surely your turning of things upside down
shall be esteemed as the potter's clay,
for shall the work say of him that made it,
'He made me not'?
or shall the thing framed say of him that
framed it, 'He had no understanding'?
¹⁷ Is it not yet a very little while,
and Lebanon shall be turned into a fruitful field,
and the fruitful field
shall be esteemed as a forest?
¹⁸And in that day shall the deaf hear
the words of the book,
and the eyes of the blind shall see
out of obscurity, and out of darkness.
¹⁹ The meek also shall increase their joy in the Lord,
and the poor among men shall rejoice
in the Holy One of Israel.
²⁰ For the terrible one is brought to nought,
and the scorner is consumed,
and all that watch for iniquity are cut off:
²¹ that make a man an offender for a word,
and lay a snare for him that reproveth in the gate,
and turn aside the just for a thing of nought.

²² Therefore thus saith the Lord,
  who redeemed Abraham,
    concerning the house of Jacob,
  Jacob shall not now be ashamed,
    neither shall his face now wax pale.
²³ But when he seeth his children,
    the work of mine hands, in the midst of him,
      they shall sanctify my name,
  and sanctify the Holy One of Jacob,
    and shall fear the God of Israel.
²⁴ They also that erred in spirit
  shall come to understanding,
    and they that murmured
  shall learn doctrine.

30 Woe to the rebellious children, saith the Lord,
    that take counsel, but not of me;
      and that cover with a covering,
    but not of my spirit,
      that they may add sin to sin;
² that walk to go down into Egypt,
    and have not asked at my mouth;
      to strengthen themselves
  in the strength of Pharaoh,
    and to trust in the shadow of Egypt!

³ Therefore shall the strength of Pharaoh
        be your shame,
            and the trust in the shadow of Egypt
        your confusion.
⁴ For his princes were at Zoan,
        and his ambassadors came to Hanes.
⁵ They were all ashamed of a people
        that could not profit them,
            nor be an help nor profit,
        but a shame, and also a reproach.
⁶ The burden of the beasts of the south:
        into the land of trouble and anguish,
            from whence come the young and old lion,
        the viper and fiery flying serpent,
            they will carry their riches
        upon the shoulders of young asses,
            and their treasures upon the bunches of camels,
        to a people that shall not profit them.
⁷ For the Egyptians shall help in vain,
        and to no purpose;
            therefore have I cried concerning this,
        'Their strength is to sit still.'
⁸ Now go, write it before them in a table,
        and note it in a book,
            that it may be for the time to come
        for ever and ever:
⁹ that this is a rebellious people, lying children,
        children that will not hear the law of the Lord;

¹⁰ which say to the seers, 'See not', and to the prophets,
      'Prophesy not unto us right things,
   speak unto us smooth things, prophesy deceits.
¹¹ Get you out of the way, turn aside out of the path,
     cause the Holy One of Israel
        to cease from before us.'
¹² Wherefore thus saith the Holy One of Israel,
     Because ye despise this word,
        and trust in oppression and perverseness,
     and stay thereon;
¹³ therefore this iniquity shall be to you
     as a breach ready to fall, swelling out in a high wall,
        whose breaking cometh
   suddenly at an instant.
¹⁴ And he shall break it
     as the breaking of the potters' vessel
        that is broken in pieces; he shall not spare:
   so that there shall not be found
     in the bursting of it a sherd
   to take fire from the hearth,
       or to take water withal out of the pit.
¹⁵ For thus saith the Lord God,
   the Holy One of Israel:
      In returning and rest shall ye be saved;
   in quietness and in confidence
      shall be your strength; and ye would not.
¹⁶ But ye said, 'No; for we will flee upon horses';
   therefore shall ye flee, and,

'We will ride upon the swift';
　　therefore shall they that pursue you
　　　　be swift.
¹⁷One thousand shall flee at the rebuke of one;
　　at the rebuke of five shall ye flee:
　　　　till ye be left as a beacon
　　upon the top of a mountain,
　　　　and as an ensign on an hill.
¹⁸And therefore will the Lord wait,
　　that he may be gracious unto you,
　　　　and therefore will he be exalted,
　　that he may have mercy upon you,
　　　　for the Lord is a God of judgment:
　　blessed are all they that wait for him.
¹⁹ For the people shall dwell in Zion at Jerusalem:
　　thou shalt weep no more.
　　　　He will be very gracious unto thee
　　at the voice of thy cry;
　　　　when he shall hear it, he will answer thee.
²⁰And though the Lord give you
　　the bread of adversity, and the water of affliction,
　　　　yet shall not thy teachers be removed
　　into a corner any more,
　　　　but thine eyes shall see thy teachers:
²¹and thine ears shall hear a word behind thee,
　　saying, 'This is the way, walk ye in it',
　　　　when ye turn to the right hand,
　　and when ye turn to the left.

²² Ye shall defile also the covering of
　thy graven images of silver,
　　and the ornament of
　thy molten images of gold:
　　thou shalt cast them away
　as a menstruous cloth;
　　thou shalt say unto it, 'Get thee hence.'
²³ Then shall he give the rain of thy seed,
　that thou shalt sow the ground withal;
　　and bread of the increase of the earth,
　and it shall be fat and plenteous:
　　in that day shall thy cattle feed in large pastures.
²⁴ The oxen likewise and the young asses
　that ear the ground shall eat clean provender,
　　which hath been winnowed
　with the shovel and with the fan.
²⁵ And there shall be upon every high mountain,
　and upon every high hill,
　　rivers and streams of waters
　in the day of the great slaughter,
　　when the towers fall.
²⁶ Moreover the light of the moon
　shall be as the light of the sun,
　　and the light of the sun shall be sevenfold,
　as the light of seven days,
　　in the day that the Lord bindeth up
　the breach of his people,
　　and healeth the stroke of their wound.

²⁷ Behold, the name of the Lord cometh from far,
    burning with his anger,
        and the burden thereof is heavy:
    his lips are full of indignation,
        and his tongue as a devouring fire.
²⁸ And his breath, as an overflowing stream,
        shall reach to the midst of the neck,
    to sift the nations with the sieve of vanity;
        and there shall be a bridle
    in the jaws of the people,
        causing them to err.
²⁹ Ye shall have a song, as in the night
    when a holy solemnity is kept;
        and gladness of heart,
    as when one goeth with a pipe to come into
        the mountain of the Lord,
    to the mighty One of Israel.
³⁰ And the Lord shall cause his glorious voice
    to be heard,
        and shall shew the lighting down of his arm,
    with the indignation of his anger,
        and with the flame of a devouring fire,
    with scattering, and tempest,
        and hailstones.
³¹ For through the voice of the Lord
    shall the Assyrian be beaten down,
        which smote with a rod.

³²And in every place
    where the grounded staff shall pass,
        which the Lord shall lay upon him,
    it shall be with tabrets and harps;
        and in battles of shaking
    will he fight with it.
³³ For Tophet is ordained of old;
    yea, for the king it is prepared;
        he hath made it deep and large:
    the pile thereof is fire and much wood;
        the breath of the Lord,
    like a stream of brimstone, doth kindle it.

31

Woe to them that go down to Egypt for help;
    and stay on horses, and trust in chariots,
        because they are many;
    and in horsemen, because they are very strong;
        but they look not unto the Holy One of Israel,
    neither seek the Lord!
² Yet he also is wise, and will bring evil,
    and will not call back his words,
        but will arise against the house
    of the evildoers,
        and against the help
    of them that work iniquity.
³ Now the Egyptians are men, and not God;
    and their horses flesh, and not spirit.

When the Lord shall stretch out his hand,
both he that helpeth shall fall,
and he that is holpen shall fall down,
and they all shall fail together.
4 For thus hath the Lord spoken unto me,
Like as the lion and the young lion
roaring on his prey when a multitude
of shepherds is called forth against him,
he will not be afraid of their voice,
nor abase himself for the noise of them:
so shall the Lord of hosts come down to fight
for mount Zion, and for the hill thereof.
5 As birds flying, so will the Lord of hosts
defend Jerusalem;
defending also he will deliver it;
and passing over he will preserve it.
6 Turn ye unto him from whom
the children of Israel have deeply revolted.
7 For in that day every man shall cast away
his idols of silver, and his idols of gold,
which your own hands have made
unto you for a sin.
8 Then shall the Assyrian fall with the sword,
not of a mighty man;
and the sword, not of a mean man,
shall devour him;
but he shall flee from the sword,
and his young men shall be discomfited.

⁹And he shall pass over to his strong hold for fear,
   and his princes shall be afraid of the ensign,
      saith the Lord, whose fire is in Zion,
      and his furnace in Jerusalem.

32 Behold, a king shall reign in righteousness,
   and princes shall rule in judgment.
²And a man shall be
   as an hiding place from the wind,
      and a covert from the tempest;
   as rivers of water in a dry place,
      as the shadow of a great rock in a weary land.
³And the eyes of them that see shall not be dim,
   and the ears of them that hear shall hearken.
⁴The heart also of the rash
   shall understand knowledge,
      and the tongue of the stammerers
   shall be ready to speak plainly.
⁵The vile person shall be no more called liberal,
   nor the churl said to be bountiful.
⁶For the vile person will speak villany,
   and his heart will work iniquity,
      to practise hypocrisy,
   and to utter error against the Lord,
      to make empty the soul of the hungry,
   and he will cause
      the drink of the thirsty to fail.

⁷ The instruments also of the churl are evil:
 he deviseth wicked devices
  to destroy the poor with lying words,
 even when the needy speaketh right.
⁸ But the liberal deviseth liberal things;
 and by liberal things shall he stand.
⁹ Rise up, ye women that are at ease;
 hear my voice, ye careless daughters;
  give ear unto my speech.
¹⁰ Many days and years shall ye be troubled,
 ye careless women, for the vintage shall fail,
  the gathering shall not come.
¹¹ Tremble, ye women that are at ease;
 be troubled, ye careless ones:
  strip you, and make you bare,
 and gird sackcloth upon your loins.
¹² They shall lament for the teats,
 for the pleasant fields, for the fruitful vine.
¹³ Upon the land of my people shall come up
 thorns and briers; yea,
  upon all the houses of joy in the joyous city;
¹⁴ because the palaces shall be forsaken;
 the multitude of the city shall be left;
  the forts and towers shall be for dens for ever,
 a joy of wild asses, a pasture of flocks;
¹⁵ until the spirit be poured upon us from on high,
 and the wilderness be a fruitful field,
  and the fruitful field be counted for a forest.

¹⁶ Then judgment shall dwell in the wilderness,
and righteousness remain in the fruitful field.
¹⁷ And the work of righteousness shall be peace;
and the effect of righteousness quietness
and assurance for ever.
¹⁸ And my people shall dwell
in a peaceable habitation,
and in sure dwellings,
and in quiet resting places;
¹⁹ when it shall hail, coming down on the forest;
and the city shall be low in a low place.
²⁰ Blessed are ye that sow beside all waters,
that send forth thither
the feet of the ox and the ass.

33 Woe to thee that spoilest,
and thou wast not spoiled;
and dealest treacherously,
and they dealt not treacherously with thee!
When thou shalt cease to spoil,
thou shalt be spoiled;
and when thou shalt make an end
to deal treacherously,
they shall deal treacherously with thee.
² O Lord, be gracious unto us;
we have waited for thee:

       be thou their arm every morning,
       our salvation also in the time of trouble.
³At the noise of the tumult the people fled;
     at the lifting up of thyself
       the nations were scattered.
⁴And your spoil shall be gathered
     like the gathering of the caterpiller:
       as the running to and fro of locusts
     shall he run upon them.
⁵The Lord is exalted; for he dwelleth on high:
     he hath filled Zion with judgment
       and righteousness.
⁶And wisdom and knowledge shall be the stability
     of thy times, and strength of salvation:
       the fear of the Lord is his treasure.
⁷Behold, their valiant ones shall cry without:
     the ambassadors of peace shall weep bitterly.
⁸The highways lie waste,
     the wayfaring man ceaseth:
       he hath broken the covenant,
     he hath despised the cities,
       he regardeth no man.
⁹The earth mourneth and languisheth;
     Lebanon is ashamed and hewn down;
       Sharon is like a wilderness;
     and Bashan and Carmel shake off their fruits.
¹⁰'Now will I rise,' saith the Lord;
     'now will I be exalted; now will I lift up myself.

¹¹ Ye shall conceive chaff, ye shall bring forth stubble;
   your breath, as fire, shall devour you.
¹² And the people shall be as the burnings of lime:
   as thorns cut up shall they be burned in the fire.'
¹³ Hear, ye that are far off, what I have done;
   and, ye that are near, acknowledge my might.
¹⁴ The sinners in Zion are afraid;
   fearfulness hath surprised the hypocrites.
      Who among us shall dwell with
   the devouring fire?
      Who among us shall dwell with
   everlasting burnings?
¹⁵ He that walketh righteously,
   and speaketh uprightly;
      he that despiseth the gain of oppressions,
   that shaketh his hands from holding of bribes,
      that stoppeth his ears from hearing of blood,
   and shutteth his eyes from seeing evil;
¹⁶ he shall dwell on high:
   his place of defence
      shall be the munitions of rocks:
   bread shall be given him;
      his waters shall be sure.
¹⁷ Thine eyes shall see the king in his beauty:
   they shall behold the land that is very far off.
¹⁸ Thine heart shall meditate terror.
   Where is the scribe? Where is the receiver?

Where is he that counted the towers?
¹⁹ Thou shalt not see a fierce people,
a people of a deeper speech
than thou canst perceive;
of a stammering tongue,
that thou canst not understand.
²⁰ Look upon Zion, the city of our solemnities:
thine eyes shall see Jerusalem a quiet habitation,
a tabernacle that shall not be taken down;
not one of the stakes thereof
shall ever be removed,
neither shall any of the cords thereof
be broken.
²¹ But there the glorious Lord will be unto us
a place of broad rivers and streams;
wherein shall go no galley with oars,
neither shall gallant ship pass thereby.
²² For the Lord is our judge, the Lord is our lawgiver,
the Lord is our king; he will save us.
²³ Thy tacklings are loosed;
they could not well strengthen their mast,
they could not spread the sail:
then is the prey of a great spoil divided;
the lame take the prey.
²⁴ And the inhabitant shall not say, 'I am sick':
the people that dwell therein
shall be forgiven their iniquity.

34 Come near, ye nations, to hear;
and hearken, ye people: let the earth hear,
and all that is therein; the world,
and all things that come forth of it.
² For the indignation of the Lord is upon all nations,
and his fury upon all their armies:
he hath utterly destroyed them,
he hath delivered them to the slaughter.
³ Their slain also shall be cast out,
and their stink shall come up
out of their carcases,
and the mountains shall be melted
with their blood.
⁴ And all the host of heaven shall be dissolved,
and the heavens shall be rolled together
as a scroll;
and all their host shall fall down,
as the leaf falleth off from the vine,
and as a falling fig from the fig tree.
⁵ For my sword shall be bathed in heaven:
behold, it shall come down upon Idumea,
and upon the people of my curse,
to judgment.
⁶ The sword of the Lord is filled with blood,
it is made fat with fatness,
and with the blood of lambs and goats,
with the fat of the kidneys of rams,
for the Lord hath a sacrifice in Bozrah,
and a great slaughter in the land of Idumea.

⁷And the unicorns shall come down with them,
   and the bullocks with the bulls;
      and their land shall be soaked with blood,
      and their dust made fat with fatness.
⁸For it is the day of the Lord's vengeance,
   and the year of recompences
      for the controversy of Zion.
⁹And the streams thereof shall be turned into pitch,
   and the dust thereof into brimstone,
      and the land thereof
      shall become burning pitch.
¹⁰It shall not be quenched night nor day;
   the smoke thereof shall go up for ever:
      from generation to generation
      it shall lie waste;
         none shall pass through
      it for ever and ever.
¹¹But the cormorant and the bittern shall possess it;
   the owl also and the raven shall dwell in it;
      and he shall stretch out upon it
      the line of confusion, and the stones
         of emptiness.
¹²They shall call the nobles thereof to the kingdom,
   but none shall be there,
      and all her princes shall be nothing.
¹³And thorns shall come up in her palaces,
   nettles and brambles in the fortresses thereof;
      and it shall be an habitation of dragons,
      and a court for owls.

¹⁴ The wild beasts of the desert shall also meet
    with the wild beasts of the island,
        and the satyr shall cry to his fellow;
    the screech owl also shall rest there,
        and find for herself a place of rest.
¹⁵ There shall the great owl make her nest,
    and lay, and hatch,
        and gather under her shadow;
    there shall the vultures also be gathered,
        every one with her mate.
¹⁶ Seek ye out of the book of the Lord, and read:
    no one of these shall fail,
        none shall want her mate;
    for my mouth it hath commanded,
        and his spirit it hath gathered them.
¹⁷ And he hath cast the lot for them,
    and his hand hath divided it unto them by line:
        they shall possess it for ever,
    from generation to generation
        shall they dwell therein.

35 The wilderness and the solitary place
    shall be glad for them;
        and the desert shall rejoice,
    and blossom as the rose.
² It shall blossom abundantly,
    and rejoice even with joy and singing:

the glory of Lebanon shall be given unto it,
the excellency of Carmel and Sharon,
they shall see the glory of the Lord,
and the excellency of our God.
³ Strengthen ye the weak hands,
and confirm the feeble knees.
⁴ Say to them that are of a fearful heart,
'Be strong, fear not:
behold, your God will come with vengeance,
even God with a recompence;
he will come and save you.'
⁵ Then the eyes of the blind shall be opened,
and the ears of the deaf shall be unstopped.
⁶ Then shall the lame man leap as an hart,
and the tongue of the dumb sing,
for in the wilderness shall waters break out,
and streams in the desert.
⁷ And the parched ground shall become a pool,
and the thirsty land springs of water:
in the habitation of dragons,
where each lay,
shall be grass with reeds and rushes.
⁸ And an highway shall be there, and a way,
and it shall be called 'The way of holiness';
the unclean shall not pass over it;
but it shall be for those:
the wayfaring men, though fools,
shall not err therein.

⁹ No lion shall be there,
  nor any ravenous beast shall go up thereon,
    it shall not be found there;
  but the redeemed shall walk there.
¹⁰ And the ransomed of the Lord shall return,
  and come to Zion with songs and
    everlasting joy upon their heads:
  they shall obtain joy and gladness,
    and sorrow and sighing shall flee away.

36 Now it came to pass in the fourteenth year
    of king Hezekiah,
      that Sennacherib king of Assyria
    came up against all the defenced cities of Judah,
      and took them.
² And the king of Assyria sent Rabshakeh
    from Lachish to Jerusalem
      unto king Hezekiah with a great army.
    And he stood by the conduit of the upper pool
      in the highway of the fuller's field.
³ Then came forth unto him Eliakim, Hilkiah's son,
    which was over the house, and Shebna the scribe,
      and Joah, Asaph's son, the recorder.
⁴ And Rabshakeh said unto them,
    'Say ye now to Hezekiah,
      Thus saith the great king,

the king of Assyria,
What confidence is this wherein thou trustest?
[5] I say, sayest thou, (but they are but vain words)
I have counsel and strength for war:
now on whom dost thou trust,
that thou rebellest against me?
[6] Lo, thou trustest in the staff of this broken reed,
on Egypt;
whereon if a man lean,
it will go into his hand, and pierce it:
so is Pharaoh king of Egypt
to all that trust in him.
[7] But if thou say to me,
"We trust in the Lord our God"
is it not he, whose high places
and whose altars Hezekiah hath taken away,
and said to Judah and to Jerusalem,
"Ye shall worship before this altar"?
[8] Now therefore give pledges, I pray thee,
to my master the king of Assyria,
and I will give thee two thousand horses,
if thou be able on thy part
to set riders
upon them.
[9] How then wilt thou turn away the face of
one captain of the least of my master's servants,
and put thy trust on Egypt for chariots
and for horsemen?

¹⁰And am I now come up without the Lord
    against this land to destroy it?
        The Lord said unto me, 'Go up against this land,
        and destroy it.'
¹¹Then said Eliakim and Shebna and Joah
    unto Rabshakeh,
        'Speak, I pray thee, unto thy servants
    in the Syrian language, for we understand it;
        and speak not to us in the Jews' language,
    in the ears of the people that are on the wall.'
¹²But Rabshakeh said,
        'Hath my master sent me to thy master
            and to thee to speak these words?
        Hath he not sent me to the men
            that sit upon the wall,
        that they may eat their own dung,
            and drink their own piss with you?'
¹³Then Rabshakeh stood, and cried with a loud voice
    in the Jews' language, and said,
        'Hear ye the words of the great king,
        the king of Assyria.
¹⁴Thus saith the king, "Let not Hezekiah deceive you,
    for he shall not be able to deliver you.
¹⁵Neither let Hezekiah make you trust in the Lord,
    saying, 'The Lord will surely deliver us:
        this city shall not be delivered
    into the hand of the king of Assyria."
¹⁶Hearken not to Hezekiah,

for thus saith the king of Assyria,

"Make an agreement with me by a present,
and come out to me: and eat ye every one of his
vine,
and every one of his fig tree, and drink ye every
one
the waters of his own cistern,
¹⁷ until I come and take you away
to a land like your own land,
a land of corn and wine,
a land of bread and vineyards.
¹⁸ Beware lest Hezekiah persuade you, saying,
The Lord will deliver us.

Hath any of the gods of the nations
delivered his land out of the hand
of the king of Assyria?
¹⁹ Where are the gods of Hamath and Arphad?
Where are the gods of Sepharvaim?
And have they delivered Samaria
out of my hand?
²⁰ Who are they among all the gods of these lands,
that have delivered their land out of my hand,
that the Lord should deliver Jerusalem
out of my hand?"'
²¹ But they held their peace,
and answered him not a word;
for the king's commandment was, saying,
'Answer him not.'

²² Then came Eliakim, the son of Hilkiah,
  that was over the household,
    and Shebna the scribe,
  and Joah, the son of Asaph, the recorder,
    to Hezekiah with their clothes rent,
  and told him the words of Rabshakeh.

37 And it came to pass, when king Hezekiah heard it,
    that he rent his clothes,
      and covered himself with sackcloth,
    and went into the house of the Lord.
  ²And he sent Eliakim, who was over the household,
    and Shebna the scribe, and the elders
      of the priests covered with sackcloth,
    unto Isaiah the prophet
      the son of Amoz.
  ³And they said unto him,
    'Thus saith Hezekiah,
      This day is a day of trouble,
    and of rebuke, and of blasphemy;
      for the children are come to the birth,
    and there is not strength to bring forth.
  ⁴It may be the Lord thy God will hear the words
    of Rabshakeh,
      whom the king of Assyria his master

hath sent to reproach the living God,
   and will reprove the words
which the Lord thy God hath heard;
   wherefore lift up thy prayer
for the remnant that is left.'
⁵ So the servants of king Hezekiah came
   to Isaiah.
⁶ And Isaiah said unto them,
   'Thus shall ye say unto your master,
      "Thus saith the Lord,
Be not afraid
   of the words that thou hast heard,
wherewith the servants of the king of Assyria
   have blasphemed me.
⁷ Behold, I will send a blast upon him,
   and he shall hear a rumour,
      and return to his own land;
   and I will cause him to fall by the sword
      in his own land."'
⁸ So Rabshakeh returned, and found the king of
   Assyria warring against Libnah,
      for he had heard
   that he was departed from Lachish.
⁹ And he heard say concerning
   Tirhakah king of Ethiopia,
      'He is come forth to make war with thee.'
   And when he heard it,
      he sent messengers to Hezekiah, saying,

¹⁰ 'Thus shall ye speak to Hezekiah king of Judah,
  saying, "Let not thy God,
    in whom thou trustest, deceive thee, saying,
  Jerusalem shall not be given
    into the hand of the king of Assyria."
¹¹ Behold, thou hast heard
  what the kings of Assyria have done
    to all lands by destroying them utterly;
  and shalt thou be delivered?
¹² Have the gods of the nations delivered them
  which my fathers have destroyed,
    as Gozan, and Haran, and Rezeph,
  and the children of Eden which were in Telassar?
¹³ Where is the king of Hamath,
  and the king of Arphad,
    and the king of the city of Sepharvaim,
  Hena, and Ivah?'
¹⁴ And Hezekiah received the letter
  from the hand of the messengers, and read it;
    and Hezekiah went up
  unto the house of the Lord,
    and spread it before the Lord.
¹⁵ And Hezekiah prayed unto the Lord, saying,
¹⁶ 'O Lord of hosts, God of Israel,
  that dwellest between the cherubims,
    thou art the God, even thou alone,
  of all the kingdoms of the earth:
    thou hast made heaven and earth.

¹⁷ Incline thine ear, O Lord, and hear;
    open thine eyes, O Lord, and see:
        and hear all the words of Sennacherib,
        which hath sent to reproach the living God.
¹⁸ Of a truth, Lord, the kings of Assyria have laid
    waste
        all the nations, and their countries,
¹⁹ and have cast their gods into the fire;
    for they were no gods,
        but the work of men's hands, wood and stone:
        therefore they have destroyed them.
²⁰ Now therefore, O Lord our God,
    save us from his hand,
        that all the kingdoms of the earth
        may know that thou art the Lord, even thou only.'
²¹ Then Isaiah the son of Amoz sent unto Hezekiah,
    saying, 'Thus saith the Lord God of Israel,
        Whereas thou hast prayed to me against
        Senacherib king of Assyria:
²² this is the word which the Lord hath spoken
    concerning him.
        The virgin, the daughter of Zion,
        hath despised thee, and laughed thee to scorn;
            the daughter of Jerusalem
        hath shaken her head at thee.
²³ Whom hast thou reproached and blasphemed?
    And against whom hast thou exalted thy voice,
        and lifted up thine eyes on high?
    Even against the Holy One of Israel.

²⁴ By thy servants hast thou reproached the Lord,
    and hast said, "By the multitude of my chariots
        am I come up to the height of the mountains,
    to the sides of Lebanon;
        and I will cut down the tall cedars thereof,
    and the choice fir trees thereof;
        and I will enter into the height of his border,
    and the forest of his Carmel.
²⁵ I have digged, and drunk water;
    and with the sole of my feet have I dried up
        all the rivers of the besieged places."
²⁶ Hast thou not heard long ago, how I have done it;
    and of ancient times, that I have formed it?
        Now have I brought it to pass,
    that thou shouldest be to lay waste
        defenced cities into ruinous heaps.
²⁷ Therefore their inhabitants were of small power,
    they were dismayed and confounded:
        they were as the grass of the field,
    and as the green herb,
        as the grass on the housetops,
    and as corn blasted before it be grown up.
²⁸ But I know thy abode, and thy going out,
    and thy coming in, and thy rage against me.
²⁹ Because thy rage against me,
    and thy tumult, is come up into mine ears,
        therefore will I put my hook in thy nose,
    and my bridle in thy lips,

and I will turn thee back
by the way by which thou camest.
³⁰And this shall be a sign unto thee.
Ye shall eat this year such as growth of itself;
and the second year
that which springeth of the same;
and in the third year sow ye, and reap,
and plant vineyards, and eat the fruit thereof.
³¹And the remnant that is escaped
of the house of Judah
shall again take root downward,
and bear fruit upward;
³²for out of Jerusalem shall go forth a remnant,
and they that escape out of mount Zion:
the zeal of the Lord of hosts shall do this.
³³Therefore thus saith the Lord
concerning the king of Assyria,
he shall not come into this city,
nor shoot an arrow there,
nor come before it with shields,
nor cast a bank against it.
³⁴By the way that he came,
by the same shall he return,
and shall not come into this city,
saith the Lord.
³⁵For I will defend this city
to save it for mine own sake,
and for my servant David's sake.'

³⁶ Then the angel of the Lord went forth,
and smote in the camp of the Assyrians
a hundred and fourscore and five thousand;
and when they arose early in the morning,
behold, they were all dead corpses.
³⁷ So Sennacherib king of Assyria departed,
and went and returned,
and dwelt at Nineveh.
³⁸ And it came to pass, as he was worshipping
in the house of Nisroch his god,
that Adrammelech and Sharezer his sons
smote him with the sword;
and they escaped into the land of Armenia;
and Esar-haddon his son reigned in his stead.

38 In those days was Hezekiah sick unto death.
And Isaiah the prophet the son of Amoz
came unto him, and said unto him,
'Thus saith the Lord, Set thine house in order:
for thou shalt die, and not live.'
² Then Hezekiah turned his face toward the wall,
and prayed unto the Lord,
³ and said, 'Remember now, O Lord,
I beseech thee, how I have walked before thee
in truth and with a perfect heart,
and have done that which is good in thy sight.'

And Hezekiah wept sore.
4 Then came the word of the Lord to Isaiah, saying,
5 'Go, and say to Hezekiah,
    Thus saith the Lord, the God of David thy father,
        I have heard thy prayer, I have seen thy tears:
    behold, I will add unto thy days fifteen years.
6 And I will deliver thee and this city
    out of the hand of the king of Assyria;
        and I will defend this city.
7 And this shall be a sign unto thee from the Lord,
    that the Lord will do this thing
        that he hath spoken;
8 Behold, I will bring again
    the shadow of the degrees,
        which is gone down in the sun dial of Ahaz,
    ten degrees backward.'
        So the sun returned ten degrees,
    by which degrees it was gone down.
9 The writing of Hezekiah king of Judah,
    when he had been sick,
        and was recovered of his sickness:
10 I said in the cutting off of my days,
    I shall go to the gates of the grave:
        I am deprived of the residue of my years.
11 I said, I shall not see the Lord,
    even the Lord, in the land of the living;
        I shall behold man no more
    with the inhabitants of the world.

¹² Mine age is departed, and is removed from me
   as a shepherd's tent;
      I have cut off like a weaver my life;
      he will cut me off with pining sickness;
         from day even to night
      wilt thou make an end of me.
¹³ I reckoned till morning, that,
      as a lion, so will he break all my bones:
         from day even to night
      wilt thou make an end of me.
¹⁴ Like a crane or a swallow, so did I chatter;
      I did mourn as a dove.
         Mine eyes fail with looking upward:
      O Lord, I am oppressed;
         undertake for me.
¹⁵ What shall I say? He hath both spoken unto me,
      and himself hath done it:
         I shall go softly all my years in the
      bitterness of my soul.
¹⁶ O Lord, by these things men live,
      and in all these things is the life of my spirit:
      so wilt thou recover me,
         and make me to live.
¹⁷ Behold, for peace I had great bitterness;
      but thou hast in love to my soul
         delivered it from the pit of corruption;
      for thou hast cast all my sins behind thy back.

¹⁸ For the grave cannot praise thee,
  death can not celebrate thee:
    they that go down into the pit
  cannot hope for thy truth.
¹⁹ The living, the living, he shall praise thee,
  as I do this day:
    the father to the children
  shall make known thy truth.
²⁰ The Lord was ready to save me;
  therefore we will sing my songs
    to the stringed instruments
  all the days of our life
    in the house of the Lord.
²¹ For Isaiah had said, 'Let them take a lump of figs,
  and lay it for a plaister
    upon the boil,
  and he shall recover.'
²² Hezekiah also had said,
    'What is the sign that I shall go up
      to the house of the Lord?'

39 At that time Merodach-baladan,
   the son of Baladan, king of Babylon,
     sent letters and a present to Hezekiah
   for he had heard that he had been sick,
     and was recovered.

²And Hezekiah was glad of them,
　　and shewed them the house
　　　　of his precious things,
　　the silver, and the gold, and the spices,
　　　　and the precious ointment,
　　and all the house of his armour,
　　　　and all that was found in his treasures:
　　there was nothing in his house,
　　　　nor in all his dominion,
　　that Hezekiah shewed them not.
³ Then came Isaiah the prophet unto king Hezekiah,
　　and said unto him, 'What said these men?
　　　　and from whence came they unto thee?'
　　And Hezekiah said,
　　　　'They are come from a far country unto me,
　　even from Babylon.'
⁴ Then said he, 'What have they seen in thine house?'
　　And Hezekiah answered,
　　　　'All that is in mine house have they seen:
　　there is nothing among my treasures
　　　　that I have not shewed them.'
⁵ Then said Isaiah to Hezekiah,
　　Hear the word of the Lord of hosts:
⁶ Behold, the days come,
　　that all that is in thine house,
　　　　and that which thy fathers have laid up
　　　　in store until this day,
　　　　　　shall be carried to Babylon:

nothing shall be left, saith the Lord.
⁷And of thy sons that shall issue from thee,
    which thou shalt beget, shall they take away;
        and they shall be eunuchs
    in the palace of the king of Babylon.
⁸Then said Hezekiah to Isaiah,
    'Good is the word of the Lord
        which thou hast spoken.'
    He said moreover,
        'For there shall be peace and truth in my days.'

40 Comfort ye, comfort ye my people,
    saith your God.
²Speak ye comfortably to Jerusalem,
    and cry unto her,
        that her warfare is accomplished,
    that her iniquity is pardoned,
        for she hath received of the Lord's hand
    double for all her sins.
³The voice of him that crieth in the wilderness,
    'Prepare ye the way of the Lord,
        make straight in the desert a highway
    for our God.
⁴Every valley shall be exalted,
    and every mountain and hill shall be made low,
        and the crooked shall be made straight,
    and the rough places plain.

⁵And the glory of the Lord shall be revealed,
and all flesh shall see it together,
for the mouth of the Lord hath spoken it.'
⁶ The voice said, 'Cry.'
And he said, 'What shall I cry?'
All flesh is grass, and all the goodliness
thereof is as the flower of the field:
⁷ The grass withereth, the flower fadeth,
because the spirit of the Lord bloweth upon it:
surely the people is grass.
⁸ The grass withereth, the flower fadeth;
but the word of our God
shall stand for ever.
⁹ O Zion, that bringest good tidings,
get thee up into the high mountain;
O Jerusalem, that bringest good tidings,
lift up thy voice with strength;
lift it up, be not afraid;
say unto the cities of Judah,
'Behold your God!'
¹⁰ Behold, the Lord God will come with strong hand,
and his arm shall rule for him:
behold, his reward is with him,
and his work before him.
¹¹ He shall feed his flock like a shepherd:
he shall gather the lambs with his arm,
and carry them in his bosom,
and shall gently lead those
that are with young.

¹² Who hath measured the waters
in the hollow of his hand,
and meted out heaven with the span,
and comprehended the dust of the earth
in a measure,
and weighed the mountains in scales,
and the hills in a balance?
¹³ Who hath directed the Spirit of the Lord,
or being his counsellor hath taught him?
¹⁴ With whom took he counsel,
and who instructed him,
and taught him in the path of judgment,
and taught him knowledge,
and shewed to him
the way of understanding?
¹⁵ Behold, the nations are as a drop of a bucket,
and are counted as the small dust of the balance:
behold, he taketh up the isles
as a very little thing.
¹⁶ And Lebanon is not sufficient to burn,
nor the beasts thereof sufficient
for a burnt offering.
¹⁷ All nations before him are as nothing;
and they are counted to him less than nothing,
and vanity.
¹⁸ To whom then will ye liken God?
Or what likeness will ye compare
unto him?

¹⁹ The workman melteth a graven image,
>> and the goldsmith spreadeth it over with gold,
>>> and casteth silver chains.
²⁰ He that is so impoverished that he hath no oblation
>> chooseth a tree that will not rot;
>>> he seeketh unto him a cunning workman
>> to prepare a graven image,
>>> that shall not be moved.
²¹ Have ye not known? Have ye not heard?
>> Hath it not been told you from the beginning?
>>> Have ye not understood
>> from the foundations of the earth?
²² It is he that sitteth upon the circle of the earth,
>> and the inhabitants thereof are as grasshoppers;
>>> that stretcheth out the heavens as a curtain,
>> and spreadeth them out as a tent to dwell in;
²³ that bringeth the princes to nothing;
>> he maketh the judges of the earth as vanity.
²⁴ Yea, they shall not be planted;
>> yea, they shall not be sown;
>>> yea, their stock
>> shall not take root in the earth;
>>> and he shall also blow upon them,
>> and they shall wither,
>>> and the whirlwind
>> shall take them away as stubble.
²⁵ To whom then will ye liken me, or shall I be equal?
>> saith the Holy One.
²⁶ Lift up your eyes on high,

and behold who hath created these things,
   that bringeth out their host by number:
he calleth them all by names
   by the greatness of his might,
for that he is strong in power; not one faileth.
²⁷ Why sayest thou, O Jacob, and speakest, O Israel,
   'My way is hid from the Lord,
      and my judgment is passed over from my God'?
²⁸ Hast thou not known? Hast thou not heard,
   that the everlasting God, the Lord,
      the Creator of the ends of the earth,
   fainteth not, neither is weary?
      There is no searching of his understanding.
²⁹ He giveth power to the faint;
   and to them that have no might
      he increaseth strength.
³⁰ Even the youths shall faint and be weary,
   and the young men shall utterly fall:
³¹ but they that wait upon the Lord
   shall renew their strength;
      they shall mount up with wings as eagles;
   they shall run, and not be weary;
      and they shall walk, and not faint.

41

Keep silence before me, O islands;
   and let the people renew their strength:
      let them come near; then let them speak:
   let us come near together to judgment.

² Who raised up the righteous man from the east,
   called him to his foot,
      gave the nations before him,
   and made him rule over kings?
      He gave them as the dust to his sword,
   and as driven stubble to his bow.
³ He pursued them, and passed safely;
   even by the way that he had not gone
      with his feet.
⁴ Who hath wrought and done it,
   calling the generations from the beginning?
      I the Lord, the first, and with the last;
   I am he.
⁵ The isles saw it, and feared;
   the ends of the earth were afraid,
      drew near, and came.
⁶ They helped every one his neighbour;
   and every one said to his brother,
      'Be of good courage.'
⁷ So the carpenter encouraged the goldsmith,
   and he that smootheth with the hammer
      him that smote the anvil, saying,
   'It is ready for the sodering':
      and he fastened it with nails,
   that it should not be moved.
⁸ But thou, Israel, art my servant,
   Jacob whom I have chosen,
      the seed of Abraham my friend.

⁹ Thou whom I have taken from the ends of the earth,
   and called thee from the chief men thereof,
      and said unto thee, 'Thou art my servant;
   I have chosen thee, and not cast thee away.'
¹⁰ Fear thou not; for I am with thee:
   be not dismayed; for I am thy God:
      I will strengthen thee;
   yea, I will help thee; yea, I will uphold thee
      with the right hand of my righteousness.
¹¹ Behold, all they that were incensed against thee
   shall be ashamed and confounded;
      they shall be as nothing;
   and they that strive with thee shall perish.
¹² Thou shalt seek them, and shalt not find them,
   even them that contended with thee:
      they that war against thee shall be as nothing,
   and as a thing of nought.
¹³ For I the Lord thy God will hold thy right hand,
   saying unto thee, 'Fear not; I will help thee.'
¹⁴ Fear not, thou worm Jacob, and ye men of Israel;
   I will help thee, saith the Lord,
      and thy redeemer,
   the Holy One of Israel.
⁵ Behold, I will make thee a new sharp threshing
   instrument having teeth:
      thou shalt thresh the mountains,
   and beat them small,
      and shalt make the hills as chaff.

¹⁶ Thou shalt fan them,
  and the wind shall carry them away,
    and the whirlwind shall scatter them:
  and thou shalt rejoice in the Lord,
    and shalt glory in the Holy One of Israel.
¹⁷ When the poor and needy seek water,
  and there is none,
    and their tongue faileth for thirst,
  I the Lord will hear them,
    I the God of Israel will not forsake them.
¹⁸ I will open rivers in high places,
  and fountains in the midst of the valleys:
    I will make the wilderness a pool of water,
  and the dry land springs of water.
¹⁹ I will plant in the wilderness the cedar,
  the shittah tree, and the myrtle, and the oil tree;
    I will set in the desert the fir tree,
  and the pine, and the box tree together:
²⁰ that they may see, and know, and consider,
  and understand together,
    that the hand of the Lord hath done this,
  and the Holy One of Israel hath created it.
²¹ Produce your cause, saith the Lord;
  bring forth your strong reasons,
    saith the King of Jacob.
²² Let them bring them forth,
  and shew us what shall happen:
    let them shew the former things, what they be,
  that we may consider them,

and know the latter end of them;
or declare us things for to come.
²³ Shew the things that are to come hereafter,
that we may know that ye are gods:
yea, do good, or do evil,
that we may be dismayed, and behold it together.
²⁴ Behold, ye are of nothing,
and your work of nought:
an abomination is he that chooseth you.
²⁵ I have raised up one from the north,
and he shall come:
from the rising of the sun
shall he call upon my name:
and he shall come upon princes
as upon morter,
and as the potter treadeth clay.
²⁶ Who hath declared from the beginning,
that we may know?
And before-time, that we may say,
'He is righteous? Yea, there is none that sheweth,
yea, there is none that declareth,
yea, there is none that heareth your words.
²⁷ The first shall say to Zion, 'Behold, behold them:
and I will give to Jerusalem
one that bringeth good tidings.
²⁸ For I beheld, and there was no man;
even among them, and there was no counsellor,
that, when I asked of them,
could answer a word.

²⁹ Behold, they are all vanity;
their works are nothing:
their molten images are wind and confusion.

42 Behold my servant, whom I uphold;
mine elect, in whom my soul delighteth;
I have put my spirit upon him:
he shall bring forth judgment to the Gentiles.
² He shall not cry, nor lift up,
nor cause his voice to be heard in the street.
³ A bruised reed shall he not break,
and the smoking flax shall he not quench:
he shall bring forth judgment unto truth.
⁴ He shall not fail nor be discouraged,
till he have set judgment in the earth:
and the isles shall wait for his law.
⁵ Thus saith God the Lord, he that created
the heavens, and stretched them out;
he that spread forth the earth,
and that which cometh out of it;
he that giveth breath unto the people upon it,
and spirit to them that walk therein:
⁶ I the Lord have called thee in righteousness,
and will hold thine hand, and will keep thee,
and give thee for a covenant of the people,
for a light of the Gentiles,

⁷ to open the blind eyes,
    to bring out the prisoners from the prison,
        and them that sit in darkness
    out of the prison house.
⁸ I am the Lord: that is my name:
    and my glory will I not give to another,
        neither my praise to graven images.
⁹ Behold, the former things are come to pass,
    and new things do I declare:
        before they spring forth I tell you of them.
¹⁰ Sing unto the Lord a new song,
    and his praise from the end of the earth,
        ye that go down to the sea,
    and all that is therein;
        the isles, and the inhabitants thereof.
¹¹ Let the wilderness and the cities thereof
    lift up their voice,
        the villages that Kedar doth inhabit:
    let the inhabitants of the rock sing,
        let them shout from the top of the
    mountains.
¹² Let them give glory unto the Lord,
    and declare his praise in the islands.
¹³ The Lord shall go forth as a mighty man,
    he shall stir up jealousy like a man of war;
        he shall cry, yea, roar;
    he shall prevail against his enemies.

¹⁴ I have long time holden my peace;
   I have been still, and refrained myself;
      now will I cry like a travailing woman;
   I will destroy and devour at once.
¹⁵ I will make waste mountains and hills,
   and dry up all their herbs;
      and I will make the rivers islands,
   and I will dry up the pools.
¹⁶ And I will bring the blind by a way
   that they knew not;
      I will lead them in paths
   that they have not known:
      I will make darkness light before them,
   and crooked things straight. These things will I
      do unto them, and not forsake them.
¹⁷ They shall be turned back,
   they shall be greatly ashamed,
      that trust in graven images,
   that say to the molten images, 'Ye are our gods.'
¹⁸ Hear, ye deaf; and look, ye blind, that ye may see.
¹⁹ Who is blind, but my servant?
   Or deaf, as my messenger that I sent?
      Who is blind as he that is perfect,
   and blind as the Lord's servant?
²⁰ Seeing many things, but thou observest not;
   opening the ears, but he heareth not.
²¹ The Lord is well pleased
   for his righteousness' sake;

he will magnify the law,
and make it honourable.
²²But this is a people robbed and spoiled;
they are all of them snared in holes,
and they are hid in prison houses:
they are for a prey, and none delivereth;
for a spoil, and none saith, 'Restore.'
²³Who among you will give ear to this?
Who will hearken and hear for the time to come?
²⁴Who gave Jacob for a spoil, and Israel to the robbers?
Did not the Lord,
he against whom we have sinned?
For they would not walk in his ways,
neither were they obedient unto his law.
²⁵Therefore he hath poured upon him the fury
of his anger, and the strength of battle;
and it hath set him on fire round about,
yet he knew not; and it burned him,
yet he laid it not to heart.

43 But now thus saith the Lord that created thee,
O Jacob, and he that formed thee, O Israel,
Fear not, for I have redeemed thee,
I have called thee by thy name;
thou art mine.

² When thou passest through the waters,
  I will be with thee; and through the rivers,
    they shall not overflow thee:
  when thou walkest through the fire,
    thou shalt not be burned;
    neither shall the flame kindle upon thee.
³ For I am the Lord thy God, the Holy One of Israel,
  thy Saviour: I gave Egypt for thy ransom,
    Ethiopia and Seba for thee.
⁴ Since thou wast precious in my sight,
  thou hast been honourable,
    and I have loved thee:
  therefore will I give men for thee,
    and people for thy life.
⁵ Fear not, for I am with thee:
  I will bring thy seed from the east,
    and gather thee from the west;
⁶ I will say to the north, 'Give up';
  and to the south, 'Keep not back:
    bring my sons from far,
  and my daughters from the ends of the earth;
⁷ even every one that is called by my name,
  for I have created him for my glory,
    I have formed him;
    yea, I have made him.'
⁸ Bring forth the blind people that have eyes,
  and the deaf that have ears.
⁹ Let all the nations be gathered together,

and let the people be assembled:
who among them can declare this,
and shew us former things?
Let them bring forth their witnesses,
that they may be justified,
or let them hear, and say, 'It is truth.'
[10] Ye are my witnesses, saith the Lord,
and my servant whom I have chosen,
that ye may know and believe me,
and understand that I am he:
before me there was no God formed,
neither shall there be after me.
[11] I, even I, am the Lord;
and beside me there is no saviour.
[12] I have declared, and have saved,
and I have shewed,
when there was no strange god among you:
therefore ye are my witnesses,
saith the Lord, that I am God.
[13] Yea, before the day was I am he;
and there is none that can deliver
out of my hand;
I will work, and who shall let it?
[14] Thus saith the Lord, your redeemer,
the Holy One of Israel;
for your sake I have sent to Babylon,
and have brought down all their nobles,
and the Chaldeans, whose cry is in the ships.

¹⁵ I am the Lord, your Holy One,
the creator of Israel, your King.
¹⁶ Thus saith the Lord,
which maketh a way in the sea,
and a path in the mighty waters;
¹⁷ which bringeth forth the chariot and horse,
the army and the power;
they shall lie down together,
they shall not rise;
they are extinct, they are quenched as tow.
¹⁸ Remember ye not the former things,
neither consider the things of old.
¹⁹ Behold, I will do a new thing;
now it shall spring forth; shall ye not know it?
I will even make a way in the wilderness,
and rivers in the desert.
²⁰ The beast of the field shall honour me,
the dragons and the owls,
because I give waters in the wilderness,
and rivers in the desert,
to give drink to my people, my chosen.
²¹ This people have I formed for myself;
they shall shew forth my praise.
²² But thou hast not called upon me, O Jacob;
but thou hast been weary of me, O Israel.
²³ Thou hast not brought me the small cattle
of thy burnt offerings;
neither hast thou honoured me

with thy sacrifices.

I have not caused thee to serve with an offering,
nor wearied thee with incense.
²⁴ Thou hast bought me no sweet cane with money,
neither hast thou filled me
with the fat of thy sacrifices,
but thou hast made me to serve with thy sins,
thou hast wearied me with thine iniquities.
²⁵ I, even I, am he that blotteth out thy transgressions
for mine own sake,
and will not remember thy sins.
²⁶ Put me in remembrance: let us plead together:
declare thou, that thou mayest be justified.
²⁷ Thy first father hath sinned,
and thy teachers have transgressed against me.
²⁸ Therefore I have profaned
the princes of the sanctuary,
and have given Jacob to the curse,
and Israel to reproaches.

44 Yet now hear, O Jacob my servant;
and Israel, whom I have chosen:
² thus saith the Lord that made thee,
and formed thee from the womb,
which will help thee:
Fear not, O Jacob, my servant;
and thou, Jesurun, whom I have chosen.

³ For I will pour water upon him that is thirsty,
  and floods upon the dry ground:
    I will pour my spirit upon thy seed,
    and my blessing upon thine offspring.
⁴ And they shall spring up as among the grass,
  as willows by the water courses.
⁵ One shall say, I am the Lord's;
  and another shall call himself
    by the name of Jacob;
  and another shall subscribe
    with his hand unto the Lord,
  and surname himself by the name of Israel.
⁶ Thus saith the Lord the King of Israel,
  and his redeemer the Lord of hosts;
    I am the first, and I am the last;
  and beside me there is no God.
⁷ And who, as I, shall call, and shall declare it,
  and set it in order for me,
    since I appointed the ancient people?
  And the things that are coming,
    and shall come, let them shew unto them.
⁸ Fear ye not, neither be afraid:
  have not I told thee from that time,
    and have declared it?
  Ye are even my witnesses.
    Is there a God beside me?
  Yea, there is no God; I know not any.
⁹ They that make a graven image
  are all of them vanity;

and their delectable things shall not profit;
and they are their own witnesses;
they see not, nor know;
that they may be ashamed.
¹⁰ Who hath formed a god, or molten a graven image
that is profitable for nothing?
¹¹ Behold, all his fellows shall be ashamed,
and the workmen, they are of men:
let them all be gathered together,
let them stand up; yet they shall fear,
and they shall be ashamed together.
¹² The smith with the tongs both worketh in the coals,
and fashioneth it with hammers,
and worketh it with the strength of his arms:
yea, he is hungry, and his strength faileth:
he drinketh no water, and is faint.
¹³ The carpenter stretcheth out his rule;
he marketh it out with a line;
he fitteth it with planes,
and he marketh it out with the compass,
and maketh it after the figure of a man,
according to the beauty of a man;
that it may remain in the house.
¹⁴ He heweth him down cedars,
and taketh the cypress and the oak,
which he strengtheneth for himself
among the trees of the forest:
he planteth an ash,
and the rain doth nourish it.

¹⁵ Then shall it be for a man to burn;
> for he will take thereof, and warm himself;
>> yea, he kindleth it, and baketh bread;
> yea, he maketh a god, and worshippeth it;
>> he maketh it a graven image,
> and falleth down thereto.
¹⁶ He burneth part thereof in the fire;
> with part thereof he eateth flesh;
>> he roasteth roast, and is satisfied:
> yea, he warmeth himself, and saith,
>> 'Aha, I am warm, I have seen the fire.'
¹⁷ And the residue thereof he maketh a god,
> even his graven image:
>> he falleth down unto it, and worshippeth it,
> and prayeth unto it, and saith,
>> 'Deliver me; for thou art my god.'
¹⁸ They have not known nor understood;
> for he hath shut their eyes,
>> that they cannot see;
> and their hearts,
>> that they cannot understand.
¹⁹ And none considereth in his heart,
> neither is there knowledge nor understanding to say,
>> 'I have burned part of it in the fire;
> yea, also I have baked bread upon the coals thereof;
>> I have roasted flesh, and eaten it:
> and shall I make the residue thereof
>> an abomination?

Shall I fall down to the stock of a tree?'
²⁰ He feedeth on ashes:
  a deceived heart hath turned him aside,
    that he cannot deliver his soul, nor say,
  'Is there not a lie in my right hand?'
²¹ Remember these, O Jacob and Israel;
  for thou art my servant:
    I have formed thee; thou art my servant:
  O Israel; thou shalt not be forgotten of me.
²² I have blotted out, as a thick cloud,
  thy transgressions,
    and, as a cloud, thy sins:
  return unto me; for I have redeemed thee.
²³ Sing, O ye heavens; for the Lord hath done it:
  shout, ye lower parts of the earth:
    break forth into singing, ye mountains,
  O forest, and every tree therein;
    for the Lord hath redeemed Jacob,
  and glorified himself in Israel.
²⁴ Thus saith the Lord, thy redeemer,
  and he that formed thee from the womb,
    I am the Lord that maketh all things;
  that stretcheth forth the heavens alone;
    that spreadeth abroad the earth by myself;
²⁵ that frustrateth the tokens of the liars,
  and maketh diviners mad;
    that turneth wise men backward,
  and maketh their knowledge foolish;

²⁶ that confirmeth the word of his servant,
  and performeth the counsel of his messengers;
    that saith to Jerusalem,
'Thou shalt be inhabited',
      and to the cities of Judah, 'Ye shall be built,
    and I will raise up the decayed places thereof;
²⁷ that saith to the deep,
  'Be dry, and I will dry up thy rivers';
²⁸ that saith of Cyrus, 'He is my shepherd,
  and shall perform all my pleasure';
    even saying to Jerusalem,
'Thou shalt be built'; and to the temple,
      'Thy foundation shall be laid.'

45 Thus saith the Lord to his anointed, to Cyrus,
    whose right hand I have holden,
      to subdue nations before him;
    and I will loose the loins of kings,
      to open before him the two leaved gates;
    and the gates shall not be shut;
² I will go before thee,
    and make the crooked places straight:
      I will break in pieces the gates of brass,
      and cut in sunder the bars of iron;
³ and I will give thee the treasures of darkness,
    and hidden riches of secret places,
      that thou mayest know that I, the Lord,

which call thee by thy name,
   am the God of Israel.
⁴For Jacob my servant's sake, and Israel mine elect,
   I have even called thee by thy name:
      I have surnamed thee,
   though thou hast not known me.
⁵I am the Lord, and there is none else,
   there is no God beside me: I girded thee,
      though thou hast not known me;
⁶that they may know from the rising of the sun,
   and from the west,
      that there is none beside me.
   I am the Lord, and there is none else.
⁷I form the light, and create darkness:
   I make peace, and create evil:
      I the Lord do all these things.
⁸Drop down, ye heavens, from above,
   and let the skies pour down righteousness:
      let the earth open,
   and let them bring forth salvation,
      and let righteousness spring up together;
   I the Lord have created it.
⁹Woe unto him that striveth with his Maker!
   Let the potsherd strive
      with the potsherds of the earth.
   Shall the clay say to him that fashioneth it,
      'What makest thou?' or thy work,
   'He hath no hands'?

¹⁰ Woe unto him that saith unto his father,
  'What begettest thou?'
    or to the woman,
  'What hast thou brought forth?'
¹¹ Thus saith the Lord, the Holy One of Israel,
  and his Maker:
    Ask me of things to come
  concerning my sons,
    and concerning the work of my hands
  command ye me.
¹² I have made the earth, and created man upon it:
  I, even my hands,
    have stretched out the heavens,
  and all their host have I commanded.
¹³ I have raised him up in righteousness,
  and I will direct all his ways:
    he shall build my city,
  and he shall let go my captives,
    not for price nor reward,
  saith the Lord of hosts.
¹⁴ Thus saith the Lord: The labour of Egypt,
  and merchandise of Ethiopia and of the Sabeans,
    men of stature, shall come over unto thee,
  and they shall be thine: they shall come after thee;
    in chains they shall come over,
  and they shall fall down unto thee,
    they shall make supplication unto thee, saying,
  'Surely God is in thee;
    and there is none else, there is no God.'

¹⁵ Verily thou art a God that hidest thyself,
  O God of Israel, the Saviour.
¹⁶ They shall be ashamed,
  and also confounded, all of them:
    they shall go to confusion together
  that are makers of idols.
¹⁷ But Israel shall be saved in the Lord
  with an everlasting salvation:
    ye shall not be ashamed nor confounded
  world without end.
¹⁸ For thus saith the Lord that created the heavens;
  God himself that formed the earth and made it;
    he hath established it,
  he created it not in vain,
    he formed it to be inhabited:
  I am the Lord; and there is none else.
¹⁹ I have not spoken in secret,
  in a dark place of the earth:
    I said not unto the seed of Jacob,
  'Seek ye me in vain':
    I the Lord speak righteousness,
  I declare things that are right.
²⁰ Assemble yourselves and come;
  draw near together,
    ye that are escaped of the nations:
  they have no knowledge
    that set up the wood of
  their graven image,
    and pray unto a god that cannot save.

²¹Tell ye, and bring them near;

yea, let them take counsel together:

who hath declared this from ancient time?

Who hath told it from that time?

Have not I the Lord?

And there is no God else beside me;

a just God and a Saviour;

there is none beside me.

²²Look unto me, and be ye saved,

all the ends of the earth,

for I am God, and there is none else.

²³I have sworn by myself, the word is gone out

of my mouth in righteousness,

and shall not return,

'That unto me every knee shall bow,

every tongue shall swear.'

²⁴Surely, shall one say, in the Lord

have I righteousness and strength:

even to him shall men come;

and all that are incensed against him

shall be ashamed.

²⁵In the Lord shall all the seed of Israel be justified,

and shall glory.

46

Bel boweth down, Nebo stoopeth,

their idols were upon the beasts,

and upon the cattle:

your carriages were heavy loaden;
    they are a burden to the weary beast.
2 They stoop, they bow down together,
    they could not deliver the burden,
        but themselves are gone into captivity.
3 Hearken unto me, O house of Jacob,
    and all the remnant of the house of Israel,
        which are borne by me from the belly,
    which are carried from the womb;
4 and even to your old age I am he;
    and even to hoar hairs will I carry you:
        I have made, and I will bear;
    even I will carry, and will deliver you.
5 To whom will ye liken me, and make me equal
    and compare me, that we may be like?
6 They lavish gold out of the bag,
    and weigh silver in the balance,
        and hire a goldsmith; and he maketh it a god:
    they fall down, yea, they worship.
7 They bear him upon the shoulder, they carry him,
    and set him in his place, and he standeth;
        from his place shall he not remove:
    yea, one shall cry unto him,
        yet can he not answer,
    nor save him out of his trouble.
8 Remember this, and shew yourselves men;
    bring it again to mind,
        O ye transgressors.

⁹ Remember the former things of old, for I am God,
    and there is none else;
        I am God, and there is none like me,
¹⁰ Declaring the end from the beginning,
    and from ancient times
        the things that are not yet done, saying,
    'My counsel shall stand, and I will do
        all my pleasure,'
¹¹ calling a ravenous bird from the east,
    the man that executeth my counsel
        from a far country: yea, I have spoken it,
    I will also bring it to pass;
        I have purposed it, I will also do it.
¹² Hearken unto me, ye stouthearted,
    that are far from righteousness;
¹³ I bring near my righteousness;
    it shall not be far off,
        and my salvation shall not tarry;
        and I will place salvation in Zion
            for Israel my glory.

47 Come down, and sit in the dust,
    O virgin daughter of Babylon, sit on the ground:
        there is no throne,
    O daughter of the Chaldeans;
        for thou shalt no more be called
    tender and delicate.
² Take the millstones, and grind meal;

uncover thy locks, make bare the leg,
    uncover the thigh, pass over the rivers.
3 Thy nakedness shall be uncovered,
    yea, thy shame shall be seen:
        I will take vengeance,
    and I will not meet thee as a man.
4 As for our redeemer, the Lord of hosts is his name,
    the Holy One of Israel.
5 Sit thou silent, and get thee into darkness,
    O daughter of the Chaldeans,
        for thou shalt no more be called,
    'The lady of kingdoms'.
6 I was wroth with my people,
    I have polluted mine inheritance,
        and given them into thine hand:
    thou didst shew them no mercy;
        upon the ancient hast thou
    very heavily laid thy yoke.
7 And thou saidst, 'I shall be a lady for ever':
    so that thou didst not
    lay these things to thy heart,
        neither didst remember the latter end of it.
8 Therefore hear now this,
    thou that art given to pleasures,
        that dwellest carelessly,
    that sayest in thine heart,
        'I am, and none else beside me;
    I shall not sit as a widow,
        neither shall I know the loss of children,'

⁹ but these two things shall come to thee
    in a moment in one day,
        the loss of children, and widowhood:
    they shall come upon thee in their perfection
        for the multitude of thy sorceries,
    and for the great abundance
        of thine enchantments.
¹⁰ For thou hast trusted in thy wickedness:
    thou hast said, 'None seeth me.'
        Thy wisdom and thy knowledge,
    it hath perverted thee;
        and thou hast said in thine heart,
    'I am, and none else beside me.'
¹¹ Therefore shall evil come upon thee;
    thou shalt not know from whence it riseth:
        and mischief shall fall upon thee;
    thou shalt not be able to put it off:
        and desolation shall come upon thee
    suddenly, which thou shalt not know.
¹² Stand now with thine enchantments,
    and with the multitude of thy sorceries,
        wherein thou hast laboured from thy youth;
    if so be thou shalt be able to profit,
        if so be thou mayest prevail.
¹³ Thou art wearied in the multitude of thy counsels.
    Let now the astrologers, the stargazers,
        the monthly prognosticators, stand up,

and save thee from these things
that shall come upon thee.
¹⁴ Behold, they shall be as stubble;
the fire shall burn them;
they shall not deliver themselves
from the power of the flame:
there shall not be a coal to warm at,
nor fire to sit before it.
¹⁵ Thus shall they be unto thee
with whom thou hast laboured,
even thy merchants, from thy youth:
they shall wander every one to his quarter;
none shall save thee.

48 Hear ye this, O house of Jacob,
which are called by the name of Israel,
and are come forth
out of the waters of Judah,
which swear by the name of the Lord,
and make mention of the God of Israel,
but not in truth, nor in righteousness.
² For they call themselves of the holy city,
and stay themselves upon the God of Israel;
the Lord of hosts is his name.

³I have declared the former things
    from the beginning;
        and they went forth out of my mouth,
    and I shewed them;
        I did them suddenly, and they came to pass.
⁴Because I knew that thou art obstinate,
    and thy neck is an iron sinew,
        and thy brow brass;
⁵I have even from the beginning declared it to thee;
    before it came to pass I shewed it thee:
        lest thou shouldest say,
    'Mine idol hath done them, and my graven
        image, and my molten image,
    hath commanded them.'
⁶Thou hast heard, see all this;
    and will not ye declare it?
        I have shewed thee new things
    from this time, even hidden things,
        and thou didst not know them.
⁷They are created now, and not from the beginning;
    even before the day when
        thou heardest them not;
    lest thou shouldest say, 'Behold, I knew them.'
⁸Yea, thou heardest not; yea, thou knewest not;
        yea, from that time that thine ear
    was not opened,
        for I knew that thou wouldest deal
    very treacherously,

     and wast called a transgressor
     from the womb.
⁹ For my name's sake will I defer mine anger,
     and for my praise will I refrain for thee,
        that I cut thee not off.
¹⁰ Behold, I have refined thee,
     but not with silver;
        I have chosen thee
     in the furnace of affliction.
¹¹ For mine own sake,
     even for mine own sake, will I do it;
        for how should my name be polluted?
     And I will not give my glory
        unto another.
¹² Hearken unto me, O Jacob and Israel, my called;
     I am he; I am the first,
     I also am the last.
¹³ Mine hand also hath laid
     the foundation of the earth,
        and my right hand
     hath spanned the heavens:
        when I call unto them, they stand up
     together.
¹⁴ All ye, assemble yourselves, and hear;
     which among them hath declared these things?
        The Lord hath loved him:
     he will do his pleasure on Babylon,
        and his arm shall be on the Chaldeans.

¹⁵ I, even I, have spoken; yea, I have called him:
    I have brought him,
    and he shall make his way prosperous.
¹⁶ Come ye near unto me, hear ye this;
    I have not spoken in secret from the beginning;
        from the time that it was, there am I:
    and now the Lord God, and his Spirit,
    hath sent me.
¹⁷ Thus saith the Lord, thy Redeemer,
    the Holy One of Israel;
        I am the Lord thy God
    which teacheth thee to profit,
        which leadeth thee by the way
    that thou shouldest go.
¹⁸ O that thou hadst hearkened
    to my commandments!
        Then had thy peace been as a river,
    and thy righteousness as the waves of the sea;
¹⁹ thy seed also had been as the sand,
    and the offspring of thy bowels
        like the gravel thereof;
    his name should not have been cut off
        nor destroyed from before me.
²⁰ Go ye forth of Babylon, flee ye from the Chaldeans,
    with a voice of singing declare ye,
        tell this, utter it even to the end of the earth;
    say ye, the Lord hath redeemed his servant Jacob.
²¹ And they thirsted not when he led them

through the deserts: he caused the waters to flow
out of the rock for them: he clave the rock also,
and the waters gushed out.
²² There is no peace, saith the Lord, unto the wicked.

49 Listen, O isles, unto me;
and hearken, ye people, from far;
the Lord hath called me from the womb;
from the bowels of my mother
hath he made mention of my name.
²And he hath made my mouth like a sharp sword;
in the shadow of his hand hath he hid me,
and made me a polished shaft;
in his quiver hath he hid me;
³and said unto me,
'Thou art my servant, O Israel,
in whom I will be glorified.'
⁴Then I said, 'I have laboured in vain,
I have spent my strength for nought, and in vain:
yet surely my judgment is with the Lord,
and my work with my God.'
⁵And now, saith the Lord that formed me
from the womb to be his servant,
to bring Jacob again to him.
'Though Israel be not gathered, yet
shall I be glorious in the eyes of the Lord,
and my God shall be my strength.'

⁶And he said, 'It is a light thing
that thou shouldest be my servant
to raise up the tribes of Jacob,
and to restore the preserved of Israel:
I will also give thee for a light to the Gentiles,
that thou mayest be my salvation
unto the end of the earth.'
⁷ Thus saith the Lord, the Redeemer of Israel,
and his Holy One, to him whom man despiseth,
to him whom the nation abhorreth,
to a servant of rulers, Kings shall see
and arise, princes also shall worship,
because of the Lord that is faithful,
and the Holy One of Israel,
and he shall choose thee.
⁸ Thus saith the Lord,
In an acceptable time have I heard thee,
and in a day of salvation have I helped thee:
and I will preserve thee,
and give thee for a covenant of the people,
to establish the earth,
to cause to inherit the desolate heritages,
⁹ that thou mayest say to the prisoners, 'Go forth';
to them that are in darkness, 'Shew yourselves.'
They shall feed in the ways,
and their pastures shall be in all
high places.

¹⁰ They shall not hunger nor thirst;
    neither shall the heat nor sun smite them;
        for he that hath mercy on them
    shall lead them, even by the springs of water
        shall he guide them.
¹¹ And I will make all my mountains a way,
    and my highways shall be exalted:
¹² Behold, these shall come from far;
    and, lo, these from the north and from the west;
        and these from the land of Sinim.
¹³ Sing, O heavens; and be joyful, O earth;
    and break forth into singing, O mountains;
        for the Lord hath comforted his people,
    and will have mercy upon his afflicted.
¹⁴ But Zion said, 'The Lord hath forsaken me,
    and my Lord hath forgotten me.'
¹⁵ Can a woman forget her sucking child,
    that she should not have compassion
        on the son of her womb?
    Yea, they may forget,
        yet will I not forget thee.
¹⁶ Behold, I have graven thee
    upon the palms of my hands;
        thy walls are continually before me.
¹⁷ Thy children shall make haste;
    thy destroyers and they that made thee waste
        shall go forth of thee.

¹⁸ Lift up thine eyes round about, and behold:
   all these gather themselves together,
     and come to thee.
   As I live, saith the Lord,
     thou shalt surely clothe thee with them all,
   as with an ornament,
     and bind them on thee, as a bride doeth.
¹⁹ For thy waste and thy desolate places,
   and the land of thy destruction,
     shall even now be too narrow
   by reason of the inhabitants,
     and they that swallowed thee up
   shall be far away.
²⁰ The children which thou shalt have,
   after thou hast lost the other,
     shall say again in thine ears,
   'The place is too strait for me:
     give place to me that I may dwell.'
²¹ Then shalt thou say in thine heart,
   'Who hath begotten me these,
     seeing I have lost my children,
   and am desolate, a captive,
     and removing to and fro?
   And who hath brought up these?
     Behold, I was left alone;
   these, where had they been?'
²² Thus saith the Lord God:
   Behold, I will lift up mine hand to the Gentiles,

and set up my standard to the people;
and they shall bring thy sons in their arms,
and thy daughters shall be carried
upon their shoulders.
²³And kings shall be thy nursing fathers,
and their queens thy nursing mothers:
they shall bow down to thee
with their face toward the earth,
and lick up the dust of thy feet;
and thou shalt know that I am the Lord;
for they shall not be ashamed
that wait for me.
²⁴Shall the prey be taken from the mighty,
or the lawful captive delivered?
²⁵But thus saith the Lord:
Even the captives of the mighty
shall be taken away,
and the prey of the terrible shall be delivered,
for I will contend with him
that contendeth with thee,
and I will save thy children.
²⁶And I will feed them
that oppress thee with their own flesh;
and they shall be drunken
with their own blood, as with sweet wine;
and all flesh shall know that I the Lord
am thy Saviour and thy Redeemer,
the mighty One of Jacob.

50 Thus saith the Lord.
    Where is the bill of your mother's divorcement,
        whom I have put away?
    Or which of my creditors is it
        to whom I have sold you?
    Behold, for your iniquities
        have ye sold yourselves,
    and for your transgressions
        is your mother put away.
² Wherefore, when I came, was there no man?
    When I called, was there none to answer?
        Is my hand shortened at all,
    that it cannot redeem?
        Or have I no power to deliver?
    Behold, at my rebuke I dry up the sea,
        I make the rivers a wilderness:
    their fish stinketh, because there is no water,
        and dieth for thirst.
³ I clothe the heavens with blackness,
    and I make sackcloth their covering.
⁴ The Lord God hath given me
    the tongue of the learned,
        that I should know how to speak a word
    in season to him that is weary:
        he wakeneth morning by morning,
    he wakeneth mine ear to hear as the learned.
⁵ The Lord God hath opened mine ear,
    and I was not rebellious,

neither turned away back.

⁶ I gave my back to the smiters, and my cheeks
   to them that plucked off the hair:
      I hid not my face from shame
      and spitting.

⁷ For the Lord God will help me;
   therefore shall I not be confounded;
      therefore have I set my face like a flint,
      and I know that I shall not be ashamed.

⁸ He is near that justifieth me;
   who will contend with me? Let us stand together:
      who is mine adversary?
   Let him come near to me.

⁹ Behold, the Lord God will help me;
   who is he that shall condemn me?
      Lo, they all shall wax old as a garment;
      the moth shall eat them up.

¹⁰ Who is among you that feareth the Lord,
   that obeyeth the voice of his servant,
      that walketh in darkness, and hath no light?
   Let him trust in the name of the Lord, and stay
      upon his God.

¹¹ Behold, all ye that kindle a fire, that compass yourselves about with sparks:
      walk in the light of your fire, and in the
      sparks that ye have kindled. This shall ye have of
      mine hand;
   ye shall lie down in sorrow.

51 Hearken to me, ye that follow after righteousness,
ye that seek the Lord:

look unto the rock whence ye are hewn,
and to the hole of the pit
whence ye are digged.

[2] Look unto Abraham your father,
and unto Sarah that bare you,
for I called him alone, and blessed him,
and increased him.

[3] For the Lord shall comfort Zion;
he will comfort all her waste places;
and he will make her wilderness like Eden,
and her desert like the garden of the Lord;
joy and gladness shall be found therein,
thanksgiving, and the voice of melody.

[4] Hearken unto me, my people;
and give ear unto me, O my nation;
for a law shall proceed from me,
and I will make my judgment to rest
for a light of the people.

[5] My righteousness is near;
my salvation is gone forth,
and mine arms shall judge the people;
the isles shall wait upon me,
and on mine arm shall they trust.

[6] Lift up your eyes to the heavens,
and look upon the earth beneath;
for the heavens shall vanish away like smoke,

and the earth shall wax old like a garment,
>and they that dwell therein shall die
in like manner;
>but my salvation shall be for ever,
and my righteousness shall not be abolished.

⁷ Hearken unto me, ye that know righteousness,
the people in whose heart is my law;
>fear ye not the reproach of men,
neither be ye afraid of their revilings.

⁸ For the moth shall eat them up like a garment,
and the worm shall eat them like wool,
>but my righteousness shall be for ever,
and my salvation from generation
>to generation.

⁹Awake, awake, put on strength, O arm of the Lord;
awake, as in the ancient days,
>in the generations of old.
Art thou not it that hath cut Rahab,
>and wounded the dragon?

¹⁰Art thou not it which hath dried the sea,
the waters of the great deep;
>that hath made the depths of the sea
a way for the ransomed to pass over?

¹¹Therefore the redeemed of the Lord shall return,
and come with singing unto Zion;
>and everlasting joy shall be upon their head:
they shall obtain gladness and joy;
>and sorrow and mourning shall flee away.

¹²I, even I, am he that comforteth you;
>who art thou, that thou shouldest be afraid
>>of a man that shall die,
>and of the son of man which shall be made
>>as grass;
¹³and forgettest the Lord thy maker,
>that hath stretched forth the heavens,
>>and laid the foundations of the earth;
>and hast feared continually every day
>>because of the fury of the oppressor,
>as if he were ready to destroy?
>>And where is the fury of the oppressor?
¹⁴The captive exile hasteneth that he may be loosed,
>and that he should not die in the pit,
>>nor that his bread should fail.
¹⁵But I am the Lord thy God, that divided the sea,
>whose waves roared:
>>the Lord of hosts is his name.
¹⁶And I have put my words in thy mouth,
>and I have covered thee
>>in the shadow of mine hand,
>that I may plant the heavens,
>>and lay the foundations of the earth,
>and say unto Zion,
>>'Thou art my people.'
¹⁷Awake, awake, stand up, O Jerusalem,
>which hast drunk at the hand of the Lord

the cup of his fury;
  thou hast drunken the dregs of the cup
    of trembling, and wrung them out.
[18] There is none to guide her among all the sons
  whom she hath brought forth;
    neither is there any that taketh her
  by the hand of all the sons
    that she hath brought up.
[19] These two things are come unto thee;
  who shall be sorry for thee?
    Desolation, and destruction,
  and the famine, and the sword:
    by whom shall I comfort thee?
[20] Thy sons have fainted,
  they lie at the head of all the streets,
    as a wild bull in a net:
  they are full of the fury of the Lord,
    the rebuke of thy God.
[21] Therefore hear now this, thou afflicted,
  and drunken, but not with wine:
[22] thus saith thy Lord the Lord,
  and thy God that pleadeth the cause
    of his people.
  Behold, I have taken out of thine hand
    the cup of trembling,
  even the dregs of the cup of my fury;
    thou shalt no more drink it again.

²³ But I will put it into the hand of them
   that afflict thee; which have said to thy soul,
      'Bow down, that we may go over':
   and thou hast laid thy body as the ground,
      and as the street, to them that went over.

52 Awake, awake; put on thy strength, O Zion;
      put on thy beautiful garments, O Jerusalem,
         the holy city;
      for henceforth there shall no more come into thee
         the uncircumcised and the unclean.
² Shake thyself from the dust;
   arise, and sit down, O Jerusalem:
      loose thyself from the bands of thy neck,
   O captive daughter of Zion.
³ For thus saith the Lord:
   Ye have sold yourselves for nought;
      and ye shall be redeemed without money.
⁴ For thus saith the Lord God:
   My people went down aforetime into Egypt
      to sojourn there;
   and the Assyrian oppressed them
      without cause.
⁵ Now therefore, what have I here, saith the Lord,
      that my people is taken away for nought?
         They that rule over them make them to howl,

saith the Lord;
>> and my name continually every day
> is blasphemed.

[6] Therefore my people shall know my name;
> therefore they shall know in that day that I am he
>> that doth speak: behold, it is I.

[7] How beautiful upon the mountains
> are the feet of him that bringeth good tidings,
>> that publisheth peace;
> that bringeth good tidings of good,
>> that publisheth salvation;
> that saith unto Zion, 'Thy God reigneth!'

[8] Thy watchmen shall lift up the voice;
> with the voice together shall they sing:
>> for they shall see eye to eye,
> when the Lord shall bring again Zion.

[9] Break forth into joy, sing together,
> ye waste places of Jerusalem;
>> for the Lord hath comforted his people,
> he hath redeemed Jerusalem.

[10] The Lord hath made bare his holy arm
> in the eyes of all the nations;
>> and all the ends of the earth
> shall see the salvation of our God.

[11] Depart ye, depart ye, go ye out from thence,
> touch no unclean thing;
>> go ye out of the midst of her;
> be ye clean, that bear the vessels of the Lord.

¹² For ye shall not go out with haste, nor go by flight;
  for the Lord will go before you;
    and the God of Israel will be your reward.
¹³ Behold, my servant shall deal prudently,
  he shall be exalted and extolled, and be very high.
¹⁴ As many were astonied at thee;
  his visage was so marred more than any man,
    and his form more than the sons of men:
¹⁵ so shall he sprinkle many nations;
  the kings shall shut their mouths at him;
    for that which had not been told them
  shall they see;
    and that which they had not heard
  shall they consider.

53 Who hath believed our report?
    And to whom is the arm of the Lord revealed?
  ² For he shall grow up before him as a tender plant,
    and as a root out of a dry ground:
      he hath no form nor comeliness;
    and when we shall see him,
      there is no beauty
    that we should desire him.
  ³ He is despised and rejected of men;
    a man of sorrows, and acquainted with grief:

and we hid as it were our faces from him;
he was despised, and we esteemed him not.
⁴ Surely he hath borne our griefs,
and carried our sorrows;
yet we did esteem him stricken,
smitten of God, and afflicted.
⁵ But he was wounded for our transgressions,
he was bruised for our iniquities;
the chastisement of our peace was upon him;
and with his stripes we are healed.
⁶ All we like sheep have gone astray;
we have turned every one to his own way;
and the Lord hath laid on him
the iniquity of us all.
⁷ He was oppressed, and he was afflicted,
yet he opened not his mouth:
he is brought as a lamb to the slaughter,
and as a sheep before her shearers is dumb,
so he openeth not his mouth.
⁸ He was taken from prison and from judgment,
and who shall declare his generation?
For he was cut off out of the land of the living:
for the transgression of my people
was he stricken.
⁹ And he made his grave with the wicked,
and with the rich in his death;
because he had done no violence,
neither was any deceit in his mouth.

^{10} Yet it pleased the Lord to bruise him;
   he hath put him to grief: when thou shalt make
      his soul an offering for sin,
   he shall see his seed, he shall prolong his days,
      and the pleasure of the Lord
   shall prosper in his hand.
^{11} He shall see of the travail of his soul,
   and shall be satisfied:
      by his knowledge shall my righteous servant
   justify many; for he shall bear their iniquities.
^{12} Therefore will I divide him a portion with the great,
   and he shall divide the spoil with the strong;
      because he hath poured out his soul unto death;
   and he was numbered with the transgressors;
      and he bare the sin of many, and made
   intercession for the transgressors.

54

Sing, O barren, thou that didst not bear;
   break forth into singing, and cry aloud,
      thou that didst not travail with child;
   for more are the children of the desolate
      than the children of the married wife,
   saith the Lord.
^{2} Enlarge the place of thy tent, and let them

stretch forth the curtains of thine habitations:
>   spare not, lengthen thy cords,
>   and strengthen thy stakes;

3 for thou shalt break forth on the right hand
>   and on the left;
>
>   and thy seed shall inherit the Gentiles,
>   and make the desolate cities to be inhabited.

4 Fear not; for thou shalt not be ashamed:
>   neither be thou confounded;
>
>   for thou shalt not be put to shame;
>   for thou shalt forget the shame of thy youth,
>   and shalt not remember the reproach
>   of thy widowhood any more.

5 For thy Maker is thine husband;
>   the Lord of hosts is his name;
>
>   and thy Redeemer the Holy One of Israel;
>   the God of the whole earth shall he be called.

6 For the Lord hath called thee as a woman forsaken
>   and grieved in spirit, and a wife of youth,
>
>   when thou wast refused, saith thy God.

7 For a small moment have I forsaken thee;
>   but with great mercies will I gather thee.

8 In a little wrath I hid my face from thee
>   for a moment;
>
>   but with everlasting kindness
>   will I have mercy on thee,
>   saith the Lord thy Redeemer.

⁹ For this is as the waters of Noah unto me;
  for as I have sworn that the waters of Noah
    should no more go over the earth,
  so have I sworn that I would not be wroth
    with thee, nor rebuke thee.
¹⁰ For the mountains shall depart,
  and the hills be removed;
    but my kindness shall not depart from thee,
  neither shall the covenant of my peace
    be removed,
  saith the Lord that hath mercy on thee.
¹¹ O thou afflicted, tossed with tempest,
  and not comforted, behold,
    I will lay thy stones with fair colours,
  and lay thy foundations with sapphires.
¹² And I will make thy windows of agates,
  and thy gates of carbuncles,
    and all thy borders of pleasant stones.
¹³ And all thy children shall be taught of the Lord;
  and great shall be the peace of thy children.
¹⁴ In righteousness shalt thou be established:
  thou shalt be far from oppression;
    for thou shalt not fear:
  and from terror; for it shall not come near thee.
¹⁵ Behold, they shall surely gather together,
  but not by me:
    whosoever shall gather together against thee
  shall fall for thy sake.

¹⁶ Behold, I have created the smith
    that bloweth the coals in the fire,
        and that bringeth forth an instrument
    for his work;
        and I have created the waster to destroy.
¹⁷ No weapon that is formed against thee
    shall prosper;
        and every tongue that shall rise against thee
    in judgment thou shalt condemn.
        This is the heritage of the servants
    of the Lord,
        and their righteousness is of me,
    saith the Lord.

55 Ho, every one that thirsteth, come ye to the waters,
    and he that hath no money;
        come ye, buy, and eat;
    yea, come, buy wine and milk without money
        and without price.
² Wherefore do ye spend money
    for that which is not bread?
        And your labour for that which satisfieth not?
    Hearken diligently unto me,
        and eat ye that which is good,
    and let your soul delight itself in fatness.

³ Incline your ear, and come unto me:
>hear, and your soul shall live;
>>and I will make an everlasting covenant
>>with you, even the sure mercies of David.
⁴ Behold, I have given him for a witness to the people,
>a leader and commander to the people.
⁵ Behold, thou shalt call a nation
>that thou knowest not,
>>and nations that knew not thee
>>shall run unto thee because of the Lord thy God,
>>>and for the Holy One of Israel;
>>for he hath glorified thee.
⁶ Seek ye the Lord while he may be found,
>call ye upon him while he is near;
⁷ let the wicked forsake his way,
>and the unrighteous man his thoughts;
>>and let him return unto the Lord,
>>and he will have mercy upon him; and to our God,
>>>for he will abundantly pardon.
⁸ For my thoughts are not your thoughts,
>neither are your ways my ways,
>>saith the Lord.
⁹ For as the heavens are higher than the earth,
>so are my ways higher than your ways,
>>and my thoughts than your thoughts.
¹⁰ For as the rain cometh down,
>and the snow from heaven,
>>and returneth not thither,

but watereth the earth,
    and maketh it bring forth and bud,
that it may give seed to the sower,
    and bread to the eater;
[11] so shall my word be that goeth forth
    out of my mouth;
        it shall not return unto me void,
    but it shall accomplish that which I please,
        and it shall prosper in the thing
    whereto I sent it.
[12] For ye shall go out with joy,
    and be led forth with peace:
        the mountains and the hills shall break forth
    before you into singing,
        and all the trees of the field
    shall clap their hands.
[13] Instead of the thorn shall come up the fir tree,
    and instead of the brier
        shall come up the myrtle tree:
and it shall be to the Lord for a name,
    for an everlasting sign that shall not be cut off.

56 Thus saith the Lord:
    Keep ye judgment, and do justice;
        for my salvation is near to come,
    and my righteousness to be revealed.

² Blessed is the man that doeth this,
>> and the son of man that layeth hold on it;
>>> that keepeth the sabbath from polluting it,
>> and keepeth his hand from doing any evil.

³ Neither let the son of the stranger,
>> that hath joined himself to the Lord, speak,
>>> saying, 'The Lord hath utterly separated me
>> from his people';
>>> neither let the eunuch say,
>> 'Behold, I am a dry tree.'

⁴ For thus saith the Lord unto the eunuchs
>> that keep my sabbaths,
>>> and choose the things that please me,
>> and take hold of my covenant;

⁵ even unto them will I give in mine house
>> and within my walls
>>> a place and a name better than of sons
>> and of daughters:
>>> I will give them an everlasting name,
>> that shall not be cut off.

⁶ Also the sons of the stranger, that join themselves
>> to the Lord, to serve him,
>>> and to love the name of the Lord,
>> to be his servants, every one
>>> that keepeth the sabbath
>> from polluting it, and taketh hold of my covenant;

⁷ even them will I bring to my holy mountain,
>> and make them joyful in my house of prayer:

their burnt offerings and their sacrifices
shall be accepted upon mine altar;
for mine house shall be called an house
of prayer for all people.

[8] The Lord God which gathereth the outcasts of Israel
saith, Yet will I gather others to him,
beside those that are gathered unto him.

[9] All ye beasts of the field, come to devour,
yea, all ye beasts in the forest.

[10] His watchmen are blind: they are all ignorant,
they are all dumb dogs, they cannot bark;
sleeping, lying down, loving to slumber.

[11] Yea, they are greedy dogs
which can never have enough,
and they are shepherds
that cannot understand:
they all look to their own way,
every one for his gain, from his quarter.

[12] Come ye, say they, I will fetch wine,
and we will fill ourselves with strong drink;
and to morrow shall be as this day,
and much more abundant.

57 The righteous perisheth, and no man layeth it
to heart; and merciful men are taken away,
none considering that the righteous
is taken away from the evil to come.

²He shall enter into peace:
>they shall rest in their beds,
>>each one walking in his uprightness.
³But draw near hither, ye sons of the sorceress,
>the seed of the adulterer and the whore.
⁴Against whom do ye sport yourselves?
>Against whom make ye a wide mouth,
>>and draw out the tongue?
>Are ye not children of transgression,
>>a seed of falsehood,
⁵enflaming yourselves with idols
>under every green tree,
>>slaying the children in the valleys
>under the clifts of the rocks?
⁶Among the smooth stones of the stream
>is thy portion; they, they are thy lot:
>>even to them hast thou poured a drink offering,
>thou hast offered a meat offering.
>>Should I receive comfort in these?
⁷Upon a lofty and high mountain
>hast thou set thy bed:
>>even thither wentest thou up to offer sacrifice.
⁸Behind the doors also and the posts
>hast thou set up thy remembrance;
>>for thou hast discovered thyself
>to another than me, and art gone up;
>>thou hast enlarged thy bed,

and made thee a covenant with them;
>> thou lovedst their bed where thou sawest it.
9And thou wentest to the king with ointment,
>> and didst increase thy perfumes,
>>> and didst send thy messengers far off,
>>> and didst debase thyself even unto hell.
10 Thou art wearied in the greatness of thy way;
>> yet saidst thou not, 'There is no hope':
>>> thou hast found the life of thine hand;
>>> therefore thou wast not grieved.
11And of whom hast thou been afraid or feared,
>> that thou hast lied,
>>> and hast not remembered me,
>> nor laid it to thy heart?
>>> Have not I held my peace even of old,
>> and thou fearest me not?
12 I will declare thy righteousness, and thy works;
>> for they shall not profit thee.
13 When thou criest, let thy companies deliver thee;
>> but the wind shall carry them all away;
>>> vanity shall take them:
>> but he that putteth his trust in me
>>> shall possess the land,
>> and shall inherit my holy mountain;
14 and shall say, 'Cast ye up, cast ye up,
>> prepare the way, take up the stumbling-block
>>> out of the way of my people.'

¹⁵ For thus saith the high and lofty One
>   that inhabiteth eternity, whose name is Holy;
>>   I dwell in the high and holy place,
>   with him also that is of a contrite
>>   and humble spirit, to revive the spirit
> of the humble,
>>   and to revive the heart of the contrite ones.
¹⁶ For I will not contend for ever,
>   neither will I be always wroth
>>   for the spirit should fail before me,
>   and the souls which I have made.
¹⁷ For the iniquity of his covetousness was I wroth,
>   and smote him: I hid me, and was wroth,
>>   and he went on frowardly
>   in the way of his heart.
¹⁸ I have seen his ways, and will heal him:
>   I will lead him also, and restore comforts
>>   unto him and to his mourners.
¹⁹ I create the fruit of the lips.
>   Peace, peace to him that is far off,
>>   and to him that is near, saith the Lord;
>   and I will heal him.
²⁰ But the wicked are like the troubled sea,
>   when it cannot rest,
>>   whose waters cast up mire and dirt.
²¹ There is no peace,
>   saith my God, to the wicked.

58

Cry aloud, spare not, lift up thy voice
like a trumpet,
and shew my people their transgression,
and the house of Jacob their sins.

² Yet they seek me daily,
and delight to know my ways,
as a nation that did righteousness,
and forsook not the ordinance of their God:
they ask of me the ordinances of justice;
they take delight in approaching to God.

³ Wherefore have we fasted, say they,
and thou seest not?
Wherefore have we afflicted our soul,
and thou takest no knowledge?
Behold, in the day of your fast
ye find pleasure,
and exact all your labours.

⁴ Behold, ye fast for strife and debate,
and to smite with the fist of wickedness:
ye shall not fast as ye do this day,
to make your voice to be heard on high.

⁵ Is it such a fast that I have chosen?
A day for a man to afflict his soul?
Is it to bow down his head as a bulrush,
and to spread sackcloth and ashes under him?
Wilt thou call this a fast,
and an acceptable day to the Lord?

⁶ Is not this the fast that I have chosen?
    To loose the bands of wickedness,
        to undo the heavy burdens,
    and to let the oppressed go free,
        and that ye break every yoke?
⁷ Is it not to deal thy bread to the hungry,
    and that thou bring the poor
        that are cast out to thy house?
    When thou seest the naked,
        that thou cover him;
    and that thou hide not thyself
        from thine own flesh?
⁸ Then shall thy light break forth as the morning,
    and thine health shall spring forth speedily:
        and thy righteousness shall go before thee;
    the glory of the Lord shall be thy reward.
⁹ Then shalt thou call, and the Lord shall answer;
    thou shalt cry, and he shall say, 'Here I am.'
        If thou take away from the midst of thee
    the yoke, the putting forth of the finger,
        and speaking vanity;
¹⁰ and if thou draw out thy soul to the hungry,
    and satisfy the afflicted soul;
        then shall thy light rise in obscurity,
    and thy darkness be as the noonday:
¹¹ and the Lord shall guide thee continually,
    and satisfy thy soul in drought,
        and make fat thy bones:

and thou shalt be like a watered garden,
      and like a spring of water,
   whose waters fail not.
¹² And they that shall be of thee
   shall build the old waste places:
      thou shalt raise up the foundations
   of many generations; and thou shalt be called,
      'The repairer of the breach',
   'The restorer of paths to dwell in'.
¹³ If thou turn away thy foot from the sabbath,
   from doing thy pleasure on my holy day;
      and call the sabbath a delight,
   the holy of the Lord, honourable;
      and shalt honour him,
   not doing thine own ways,
      nor finding thine own pleasure,
      nor speaking thine own words:
¹⁴ then shalt thou delight thyself in the Lord;
   and I will cause thee to ride
      upon the high places of the earth,
   and feed thee with the heritage
      of Jacob thy father;
   for the mouth of the Lord hath spoken it.

59 Behold, the Lord's hand is not shortened,
      that it cannot save; neither his ear heavy,
         that it cannot hear.

² But your iniquities have separated between you
and your God,
and your sins have hid his face from you,
that he will not hear.
³ For your hands are defiled with blood,
and your fingers with iniquity;
your lips have spoken lies,
your tongue hath muttered perverseness.
⁴ None calleth for justice, nor any pleadeth for truth:
they trust in vanity, and speak lies;
they conceive mischief,
and bring forth iniquity.
⁵ They hatch cockatrice' eggs,
and weave the spider's web:
he that eateth of their eggs dieth,
and that which is crushed breaketh
out into a viper.
⁶ Their webs shall not become garments,
neither shall they cover themselves
with their works:
their works are works of iniquity,
and the act of violence is in their hands.
⁷ Their feet run to evil,
and they make haste to shed innocent blood:
their thoughts are thoughts of iniquity;
wasting and destruction are in their paths.
⁸ The way of peace they know not;

and there is no judgment in their goings:
>> they have made them crooked paths:
>> whosoever goeth therein shall not know peace.
⁹ Therefore is judgment far from us,
>> neither doth justice overtake us:
>>> we wait for light, but behold obscurity;
>> for brightness, but we walk in darkness.
¹⁰ We grope for the wall like the blind,
>> and we grope as if we had no eyes;
>>> we stumble at noonday as in the night;
>> we are in desolate places as dead men.
¹¹ We roar all like bears, and mourn sore like doves:
>> we look for judgment, but there is none;
>>> for salvation, but it is far off from us.
¹² For our transgressions are multiplied before thee,
>> and our sins testify against us;
>>> for our transgressions are with us;
>> and as for our iniquities, we know them;
¹³ in transgressing and lying against the Lord,
>> and departing away from our God,
>>> speaking oppression and revolt,
>> conceiving and uttering from the heart
>> words of falsehood.
¹⁴ And judgment is turned away backward,
>> and justice standeth afar off;
>>> for truth is fallen in the street, and
>> equity cannot enter.

¹⁵ Yea, truth faileth; and he that departeth from evil
maketh himself a prey:

and the Lord saw it, and it displeased him
that there was no judgment.

¹⁶ And he saw that there was no man,
and wondered that there was no intercessor:

therefore his arm brought salvation unto him;
and his righteousness, it sustained him.

¹⁷ For he put on righteousness as a breastplate,
and an helmet of salvation upon his head;

and he put on the garments of vengeance
for clothing,

and was clad with zeal as a cloke.

¹⁸ According to their deeds, accordingly he will repay,
fury to his adversaries,

recompence to his enemies;
to the islands he will repay recompence.

¹⁹ So shall they fear the name of the Lord
from the west,

and his glory from the rising of the sun.
When the enemy shall come in like a flood,

the Spirit of the Lord shall lift up a standard
against him.

²⁰ And the Redeemer shall come to Zion,
and unto them that turn from transgression
in Jacob, saith the Lord.

²¹ As for me, this is my covenant with them,

saith the Lord, my spirit that is upon thee,
    and my words which I have put in thy mouth,
shall not depart out of thy mouth,
    nor out of the mouth of thy seed,
nor out of the mouth of thy seed's seed,
    saith the Lord, from henceforth and for ever.

60 Arise, shine; for thy light is come,
    and the glory of the Lord is risen upon thee.
2 For, behold, the darkness shall cover the earth,
    and gross darkness the people,
        but the Lord shall arise upon thee,
    and his glory shall be seen upon thee.
3 And the Gentiles shall come to thy light,
    and kings to the brightness of thy rising.
4 Lift up thine eyes round about, and see:
    all they gather themselves together,
        they come to thee: thy sons shall come from far,
    and thy daughters shall be nursed at thy side.
5 Then thou shalt see, and flow together,
    and thine heart shall fear, and be enlarged;
        because the abundance of the see
    shall be converted unto thee,
        the forces of the Gentiles
    shall come unto thee.

⁶ The multitude of camels shall cover thee,
 the dromedaries of Midian and Ephah;
  all they from Sheba shall come:
 they shall bring gold and incense;
  and they shall shew forth
 the praises of the Lord.
⁷ All the flocks of Kedar
 shall be gathered together unto thee,
  the rams of Nebaioth
 shall minister unto thee:
  they shall come up with acceptance
 on mine altar,
  and I will glorify the house of my glory.
⁸ Who are these that fly as a cloud,
 and as the doves to their windows?
⁹ Surely the isles shall wait for me,
 and the ships of Tarshish first,
  to bring thy sons from far,
 their silver and their gold with them,
  unto the name of the Lord thy God,
 and to the Holy One of Israel,
  because he hath glorified thee.
¹⁰ And the sons of strangers shall build up thy walls,
 and their kings shall minister unto thee,
  for in my wrath I smote thee,
 but in my favour have I had mercy
  on thee.

¹¹ Therefore thy gates shall be open continually;
    they shall not be shut day nor night;
       that men may bring unto thee
    the forces of the Gentiles,
       and that their kings may be brought.
¹² For the nation and kingdom that will not serve thee
    shall perish;
       yea, those nations shall be utterly wasted.
¹³ The glory of Lebanon shall come unto thee,
    the fir tree, the pine tree, and the box together,
       to beautify the place of my sanctuary;
    and I will make the place of my feet glorious.
¹⁴ The sons also of them that afflicted thee shall come
    bending unto thee;
       and all they that despised thee shall bow
    themselves down at the soles of thy feet;
       and they shall call thee 'The city of the Lord',
    'The Zion of the Holy One of Israel'.
¹⁵ Whereas thou hast been forsaken and hated,
    so that no man went through thee,
       I will make thee an eternal excellency,
    a joy of many generations.
¹⁶ Thou shalt also suck the milk of the Gentiles,
    and shalt suck the breast of kings;
       and thou shalt know that I the Lord
    am thy Saviour and thy Redeemer,
       the mighty One of Jacob.

¹⁷ For brass I will bring gold,
    and for iron I will bring silver,
        and for wood brass, and for stones iron:
    I will also make thy officers peace,
        and thine exactors righteousness.
¹⁸ Violence shall no more be heard in thy land,
    wasting nor destruction within thy borders;
        but thou shalt call thy walls Salvation,
    and thy gates Praise.
¹⁹ The sun shall be no more thy light by day;
    neither for brightness
        shall the moon give light unto thee:
    but the Lord shall be
        unto thee an everlasting light,
    and thy God thy glory.
²⁰ Thy sun shall no more go down;
    neither shall thy moon withdraw itself,
        for the Lord shall be thine everlasting light,
    and the days of thy mourning shall be ended.
²¹ Thy people also shall be all righteous:
    they shall inherit the land for ever,
        the branch of my planting,
    the work of my hands,
        that I may be glorified.
²² A little one shall become a thousand, and a small
    one a strong nation:
        I the Lord will hasten it in his time.

JESUS QUOTES
THESE VV
AT BEG.
OF HIS
MINISTRY
(IN NAZA
RETH)
LK 4.
16-21

61 The Spirit of the Lord God is upon me;
    because the Lord hath anointed me to preach
        good tidings unto the meek;
    he hath sent me to bind up the brokenhearted,
        to proclaim liberty to the captives,
    and the opening of the prison to them
        that are bound;
² to proclaim the acceptable year of the Lord,
    and the day of vengeance of our God; _Jesus misses this
        to comfort all that mourn;   line out.
³ to appoint unto them that mourn in Zion,
    to give unto them beauty for ashes,
        the oil of joy for mourning,
    the garment of praise for the spirit of heaviness;
        that they might be called
    trees of righteousness, the planting of the Lord,
        that he might be glorified.
⁴And they shall build the old wastes,
    they shall raise up the former desolations,
        and they shall repair the waste cities,
    the desolations of many generations.
⁵And strangers shall stand and feed your flocks,
    and the sons of the alien shall be your plowmen
        and your vinedressers.
⁶ But ye shall be named the Priests of the Lord:
    men shall call you the Ministers of our God:
        ye shall eat the riches of the Gentiles,
    and in their glory shall ye boast yourselves.

⁷ For your shame ye shall have double;
    and for confusion they shall rejoice
        in their portion: therefore in their land
    they shall possess the double:
        everlasting joy shall be unto them.
⁸ For I the Lord love judgment,
    I hate robbery for burnt offering;
        and I will direct their work in truth,
    and I will make an everlasting covenant
        with them.
⁹ And their seed shall be known among the Gentiles,
    and their offspring among the people:
        all that see them shall acknowledge them,
    that they are the seed
        which the Lord hath blessed.
¹⁰ I will greatly rejoice in the Lord,
    my soul shall be joyful in my God;
        for he hath clothed me
    with the garments of salvation,
        he hath covered me with the robe
    of righteousness,
        as a bridegroom decketh himself
    with ornaments,
        and as a bride adorneth herself with her jewels.
¹¹ For as the earth bringeth forth her bud,
    and as the garden causeth the things
        that are sown in it to spring forth;
    so the Lord God will cause righteousness

and praise to spring forth before all
the nations.

62 For Zion's sake will I not hold my peace,
and for Jerusalem's sake I will not rest,
until the righteousness thereof
go forth as brightness, and the salvation thereof
as a lamp that burneth.
²And the Gentiles shall see thy righteousness,
and all kings thy glory;
and thou shalt be called by a new name,
which the mouth of the Lord shall name.
³Thou shalt also be a crown of glory
in the hand of the Lord,
and a royal diadem in the hand of thy God.
⁴Thou shalt no more be termed Forsaken;
neither shall thy land any more be termed
Desolate:
but thou shalt be called Hephzi-bah,
and thy land Beulah;
for the Lord delighteth in thee,
and thy land shall be married.
⁵For as a young man marrieth a virgin,
so shall thy sons marry thee: and as the bridegroom
rejoiceth over the bride,
so shall thy God rejoice over thee.

⁶ I have set watchmen upon thy walls, O Jerusalem,
    which shall never hold their peace day nor night:
        ye that make mention of the Lord,
    keep not silence,
⁷ and give him no rest, till he establish,
    and till he make Jerusalem a praise in the earth.
⁸ The Lord hath sworn by his right hand,
    and by the arm of his strength:
        Surely I will no more give thy corn
    to be meat for thine enemies;
        and the sons of the stranger
    shall not drink thy wine,
        for the which thou hast laboured;
⁹ But they that have gathered it shall eat it,
    and praise the Lord;
        and they that have brought it together
    shall drink it in the courts of my holiness.
¹⁰ Go through, go through the gates;
    prepare ye the way of the people;
        cast up, cast up the highway;
    gather out the stones;
        lift up a standard for the people.
¹¹ Behold, the Lord hath proclaimed
    unto the end of the world:
        Say ye to the daughter of Zion,
    'Behold, thy salvation cometh; behold, his
        reward is with him,
    and his work before him.'

¹²And they shall call them, 'The holy people,
the redeemed of the Lord':
and thou shalt be called,
'Sought out, A city not forsaken'.

63 Who is this that cometh from Edom,
with dyed garments from Bozrah?
This that is glorious in his apparel,
travelling in the greatness of his strength?
I that speak in righteousness,
mighty to save.
² Wherefore art thou red in thine apparel,
and thy garments like him
that treadeth in the winefat?
³ I have trodden the winepress alone;
and of the people there was none with me;
for I will tread them in mine anger,
and trample them in my fury;
and their blood shall be sprinkled
upon my garments, and I will stain all my raiment.
⁴ For the day of vengeance is in mine heart,
and the year of my redeemed is come.
⁵And I looked, and there was none to help;
and I wondered that there was none to uphold:
therefore mine own arm brought salvation
unto me; and my fury, it upheld me.

⁶And I will tread down the people in mine anger,
  and make them drunk in my fury,
    and I will bring down their strength
  to the earth.
⁷I will mention the lovingkindnesses of the Lord,
  and the praises of the Lord,
    according to all that the Lord
  hath bestowed on us, and the great goodness
    toward the house of Israel,
  which he hath bestowed on them
    according to his mercies,
  and according to the multitude
    of his lovingkindnesses.
⁸For he said: Surely they are my people,
  children that will not lie,
    so he was their Saviour.
⁹In all their affliction he was afflicted,
  and the angel of his presence saved them;
    in his love and in his pity he redeemed them;
  and he bare them, and carried them
    all the days of old.
¹⁰But they rebelled, and vexed his holy Spirit:
  therefore he was turned to be their enemy,
    and he fought against them.
¹¹Then he remembered the days of old, Moses,
  and his people, saying,
    'Where is he that brought them up
  out of the sea with the shepherd of his flock?

Where is he that put his holy Spirit
within him?
¹² That led them by the right hand of Moses
with his glorious arm,
dividing the water before them,
to make himself an everlasting name?
¹³ That led them through the deep,
as an horse in the wilderness,
that they should not stumble?'
¹⁴ As a beast goeth down into the valley,
the Spirit of the Lord caused him to rest:
so didst thou lead thy people,
to make thyself a glorious name.
¹⁵ Look down from heaven, and behold
from the habitation of thy holiness
and of thy glory:
where is thy zeal and thy strength,
the sounding of thy bowels and of thy mercies
toward me? Are they restrained?
¹⁶ Doubtless thou art our father,
though Abraham be ignorant of us,
and Israel acknowledge us not:
thou, O Lord, art our father, our redeemer;
thy name is from everlasting.
¹⁷ O Lord, why hast thou made us to err
from thy ways,
and hardened our heart from thy fear?
Return for thy servants' sake,
the tribes of thine inheritance.

¹⁸ The people of thy holiness have possessed it
  but a little while:
      our adversaries have trodden down
  thy sanctuary.
¹⁹ We are thine: thou never barest rule over them;
  they were not called by thy name.

64 Oh that thou wouldest rend the heavens,
      that thou wouldest come down,
          that the mountains might flow down
      at thy presence,
² as when the melting fire burneth,
  the fire causeth the waters to boil,
      to make thy name known to thine adversaries,
      that the nations may tremble at thy presence!
³ When thou didst terrible things
  which we looked not for, thou camest down,
      the mountains flowed down at thy presence.
⁴ For since the beginning of the world
  men have not heard, nor perceived by the ear,
      neither hath the eye seen, O God, beside thee,
  what he hath prepared for him
      that waiteth for him.
⁵ Thou meetest him that rejoiceth
  and worketh righteousness,

those that remember thee in thy ways:
behold, thou art wroth; for we have sinned;
in those is continuance,
and we shall be saved.
⁶ But we are all as an unclean thing, and all our
righteousnesses are as filthy rags;
and we all do fade as a leaf;
and our iniquities, like the wind,
have taken us away.
⁷ And there is none that calleth upon thy name,
that stirreth up himself to take hold of thee
for thou hast hid thy face from us,
and hast consumed us,
because of our iniquities.
⁸ But now, O Lord, thou art our father;
we are the clay, and thou our potter;
and we all are the work of thy hand.
⁹ Be not wroth very sore, O Lord, neither remember
iniquity for ever: behold, see, we beseech thee,
we are all thy people.
¹⁰ Thy holy cities are a wilderness,
Zion is a wilderness, Jerusalem a desolation.
¹¹ Our holy and our beautiful house, where our
fathers praised thee, is burned up with fire:
and all our pleasant things are laid waste.
¹² Wilt thou refrain thyself for these things, O Lord?
Wilt thou hold thy peace,
and afflict us very sore?

65 I am sought of them that asked not for me;
   I am found of them that sought me not:
      I said, 'Behold me, behold me,'
   unto a nation that was not called by my name.
² I have spread out my hands all the day
   unto a rebellious people,
      which walketh in a way that was not good,
   after their own thoughts;
³ a people that provoketh me to anger
   continually to my face; that sacrificeth in gardens,
      and burneth incense upon altars of brick;
⁴ which remain among the graves,
   and lodge in the monuments,
      which eat swine's flesh,
   and broth of abominable things
      is in their vessels;
⁵ which say, 'Stand by thyself, come not near to me;
   for I am holier than thou.'
      These are a smoke in my nose,
   a fire that burneth all the day.
⁶ Behold, it is written before me:
   I will not keep silence, but will recompense,
      even recompense into their bosom,
⁷ your iniquities, and the iniquities of your fathers
   together, saith the Lord,
      which have burned incense upon the mountains,
   and blasphemed me upon the hills:

therefore will I measure their former work
into their bosom.
⁸ Thus saith the Lord:
as the new wine is found in the cluster,
and one saith,
'Destroy it not; for a blessing is in it':
so will I do for my servants' sakes,
that I may not destroy them all.
⁹ And I will bring forth a seed out of Jacob,
and out of Judah an inheritor of my mountains:
and mine elect shall inherit it,
and my servants shall dwell there.
¹⁰ And Sharon shall be a fold of flocks,
and the valley of Achor a place for the herds
to lie down in,
for my people that have sought me.
¹¹ But ye are they that forsake the Lord,
that forget my holy mountain,
that prepare a table for that troop,
and that furnish the drink offering
unto that number.
¹² Therefore will I number you to the sword,
and ye shall all bow down to the slaughter:
because when I called, ye did not answer;
when I spake, ye did not hear;
but did evil before mine eyes,
and did choose that wherein I delighted not.

¹³ Therefore thus saith the Lord God:
    Behold, my servants shall eat,
        but ye shall be hungry:
    behold, my servants shall drink,
        but ye shall be thirsty:
    behold, my servants shall rejoice,
        but ye shall be ashamed.
¹⁴ Behold, my servants shall sing for joy of heart,
    but ye shall cry for sorrow of heart
        and shall howl for vexation of spirit.
¹⁵ And ye shall leave your name for a curse
    unto my chosen,
        for the Lord God shall slay thee,
    and call his servants by another name:
¹⁶ that he who blesseth himself in the earth
    shall bless himself in the God of truth;
        and he that sweareth in the earth
    shall swear by the God of truth;
        because the former troubles are forgotten,
    and because they are hid from mine eyes.
¹⁷ For, behold, I create new heavens
    and a new earth:
        and the former shall not be remembered,
    nor come into mind.
¹⁸ But be ye glad and rejoice for ever
    in that which I create;
        for, behold, I create Jerusalem a rejoicing,
    and her people a joy.

¹⁹And I will rejoice in Jerusalem,
    and joy in my people:
        and the voice of weeping shall be no more
    heard in her, nor the voice of crying.
²⁰There shall be no more thence an infant of days,
    nor an old man that hath not filled his days;
        for the child shall die an hundred years old;
    but the sinner being an hundred years old shall
        be accursed.
²¹And they shall build houses, and inhabit them;
    and they shall plant vineyards,
        and eat the fruit of them.
²²They shall not build, and another inhabit;
    they shall not plant, and another eat,
        for as the days of a tree
    are the days of my people, and mine elect
        shall long enjoy the work of their hands.
²³They shall not labour in vain,
    nor bring forth for trouble;
        for they are the seed of the blessed of
    the Lord, and their offspring with them.
²⁴And it shall come to pass,
    that before they call, I will answer;
        and while they are yet speaking, I will hear.
²⁵The wolf and the lamb shall feed together,
    and the lion shall eat straw like the bullock:
        and dust shall be the serpent's meat.
    They shall not hurt nor destroy in all
        my holy mountain, saith the Lord.

66 Thus saith the Lord: The heaven is my throne,
and the earth is my footstool:

> where is the house that ye build unto me?
> And where is the place of my rest?

² For all those things hath mine hand made,
and all those things have been, saith the Lord;

> but to this man will I look,
> even to him that is poor and of a contrite spirit,
> and trembleth at my word.

³ He that killeth an ox is as if he slew a man;
he that sacrificeth a lamb,

> as if he cut off a dog's neck;

he that offereth an oblation,

> as if he offered swine's blood;

he that burneth incense, as if he blessed an idol.

> Yea, they have chosen their own ways,
> and their soul delighteth in their abominations.

⁴ I also will choose their delusions,
and will bring their fears upon them;

> because when I called, none did answer;

when I spake, they did not hear;

> but they did evil before mine eyes,
> and chose that in which I delighted not.

⁵ Hear the word of the Lord,
ye that tremble at his word.

> Your brethren that hated you,
> that cast you out for my name's sake,
> said, 'Let the Lord be glorified,

but he shall appear to your joy',
and they shall be ashamed.
⁶A voice of noise from the city,
a voice from the temple,
a voice of the Lord that rendereth
recompence to his enemies.
⁷ Before she travailed, she brought forth;
before her pain came,
she was delivered of a man child.
⁸ Who hath heard such a thing?
Who hath seen such things?
Shall the earth be made to bring forth
in one day?
Or shall a nation be born at once?
For as soon as Zion travailed,
she brought forth her children.
⁹ Shall I bring to the birth,
and not cause to bring forth? saith the Lord.
Shall I cause to bring forth,
and shut the womb? saith thy God.
¹⁰ Rejoice ye with Jerusalem,
and be glad with her, all ye that love her:
rejoice for joy with her,
all ye that mourn for her,
¹¹ that ye may suck, and be satisfied
with the breasts of her consolations;
that ye may milk out, and be delighted
with the abundance of her glory.

¹² For thus saith the Lord.

> Behold, I will extend peace to her like a river,
>> and the glory of the Gentiles
> like a flowing stream: then shall ye suck,
>> ye shall be borne upon her sides,
> and be dandled upon her knees.

¹³ As one whom his mother comforteth,
> so will I comfort you;
>> and ye shall be comforted in Jerusalem.

¹⁴ And when ye see this, your heart shall rejoice,
> and your bones shall flourish like an herb:
>> and the hand of the Lord shall be known
> toward his servants,
>> and his indignation toward his enemies.

¹⁵ For, behold, the Lord will come with fire,
> and with his chariots like a whirlwind,
>> to render his anger with fury,
> and his rebuke with flames of fire.

¹⁶ For by fire and by his sword will the Lord
> plead with all flesh:
>> and the slain of the Lord shall be many.

¹⁷ They that sanctify themselves,
> and purify themselves in the gardens
>> behind one tree in the midst,
> eating swine's flesh, and the abomination,
>> and the mouse, shall be consumed together,
> saith the Lord.

¹⁸ For I know their works and their thoughts:
   it shall come, that I will gather all nations
      and tongues; and they shall come,
   and see my glory.
¹⁹And I will set a sign among them,
   and I will send those that escape of them
      unto the nations, to Tarshish, Pul, and Lud,
   that draw the bow, to Tubal, and Javan,
      to the isles afar off,
   that have not heard my fame,
      neither have seen my glory;
   and they shall declare my glory
      among the Gentiles.
²⁰And they shall bring all your brethren
   for an offering unto the Lord
      out of all nations upon horses,
   and in chariots, and in litters, and upon mules,
      and upon swift beasts,
   to my holy mountain Jerusalem,
      saith the Lord, as the children of Israel
   bring an offering in a clean vessel
      into the house of the Lord.
²¹And I will also take of them for priests
   and for Levites, saith the Lord.
²² For as the new heavens and the new earth,
   which I will make, shall remain before me,
      saith the Lord,
   so shall your seed and your name remain.

²³And it shall come to pass,
   that from one new moon to another,
      and from one sabbath to another,
   shall all flesh come to worship before me,
      saith the Lord.
²⁴And they shall go forth, and look upon the carcases
   of the men that have transgressed against me;
      for their worm shall not die,
   neither shall their fire be quenched;
      and they shall be an abhorring unto all flesh.